GW00326589

ROY LANCASTER

SHRUBS
Through the Seasons

ROY LANCASTER

SHRUBS Through the Seasons

HarperCollins*Publishers*

This book is dedicated
to the memory of my father
who did not live to see
his hobby become my profession
and to that of my mother
whose love and hard work
made it possible

As I have found before when venturing beyond personal experience, friends and colleagues in the horticultural profession have been more than generous with information requested for this book. They include Reg Alford, Elizabeth Braimbridge, Lynn Batdorf, the late Harry Bryce, Mike Cliff, Peter Cox, Ivan Dickings, Peter Dummer, John Elsley, John Gallagher, David Hutchinson, Kurt Kramer, Peter Moore, Alan Postill, Charles Puddle, Michael Taylor, Neil Treseder, Pat Turpin and Harry van de Laar. To all these and others with whom I have discussed shrubs during the writing of this book I extend my thanks.

I owe a special debt of gratitude to Brian Humphrey who rashly agreed to read my manuscript responding with numerous helpful comments particularly concerning methods of propagation. Allen Coombes kindly gave me permission to quote from his excellent guide *The Collingridge Dictionary of Plant Names* on the pronunciation and meaning of shrub names in this book, while my old friend and former colleague Hatton Gardner has generously prepared the index.

Considering the length of time this book has been 'on the go' and the problems and vicissitudes it has suffered I should also like to say a special thanks to the former editorial staff of Unwin Hyman especially Mary Butler, for their patience and fortitude and latterly to those of HarperCollins in particular Polly Powell and designer Caroline Hill for their professionalism. Last, but by no means least, I thank my wife Sue for typing the manuscript.

First published in 1991 by HarperCollins Publishers, London

British Library Cataloguing in Publication Data
Lancaster, Roy
Shrubs through the seasons.
1. Garden. Shrubs
I. Title
635.976

ISBN 000 412621 1

Designed by Caroline Hill

Printed and bound in Great Britain
by HarperCollins Manufacturing, Glasgow

Page 1: *Camellia* **'Inspiration'** is one of the best hybrids for general cultivation.

Page 2: *Corylus avellara* **'Cantorta'**, the curious Harry Lauder's Walking-stick.

CONTENTS

Introduction

Despite the current resurgence of perennials, shrubs are still the most popular and most commonly used of all hardy plants, in British gardens certainly. Whether used as a background, to complement other plants or as individuals, there are few gardens without them. The only thing that surprises me is that considering the rich variety now available there is still a tendency among many gardeners to stick to a fairly limited selection, often the old favourites. Now, while I am all in favour of planting well tried and reliable shrubs, especially if you are a first time gardener, I believe that gardeners should be made aware of the many new shrubs – hybrids and cultivars (garden varieties) introduced to commerce every year. Not all of these, of course, are of great merit but some at least are worth considering.

In this book I have brought together details of over 300 shrubs old and new, most of which I have seen, if not grown, in various gardens. Those which I have not seen I have included on good authority. Most are hardy throughout colder temperate climates, whilst a number of tender plants or those of borderline hardiness have been included to interest adventurous gardeners and those lucky enough to garden in mild areas or in warm pockets elsewhere. Mind you, the way the weather has been behaving in recent years and if predictions as to the climatic changes likely to occur are to be believed, then the areas suitable for such plants are expanding.

Even more unpredictable are flowering times. Those given in this book are based on observations over many years but recent winters have made nonsense of accurate forecasting. In 1990 for instance, forsythias which are traditionally spring flowering were at least a month early in many gardens and there are countless other examples. Flowering times, therefore, as well as growth rates and ultimate sizes as given in this book, should be regarded as approximate under average conditions.

I have done my best in the descriptions to offer guidance on such essentials as preferred aspect, soil and situation and this has been repeated in key form below each entry heading as a rapid check. Each featured shrub is illustrated and details provided of its botanical family, e.g. *Camellia* belongs to the family *Theaceae*. Guidance is also given on the correct pronunciation and meaning of shrub names featured, e.g. *Abelia floribunda*: a-*bel*-ee-a, after Dr Clarke Abel (1780–1826) who introduced *A. chinensis*; flo-ri-*bun*-da, free flowering.

Comments of a practical nature, such as those concerning pruning and propagation, are brief and to the point. Propagation especially, is far too large and important a subject to be adequately covered in this book. Unless otherwise stated, all shrubs described are of a deciduous nature although certain ones may retain a proportion of their leaves in a mild winter.

For British and European gardeners

The following seasonal guidelines apply:

Mid winter	January
Late Winter	February
Early spring	March
Mid spring	April
Late spring	May
Early summer	June
Mid summer	July
Late summer	August
Early autumn	September
Mid autumn	October
Late autumn	November
Early winter	December

For American gardeners

Each shrub has been designated a zone range, the lower number indicating the most northerly area where it will reliably survive the winter, and the higher number the most southerly area where it will perform consistently. However, many factors, such as altitude and degree of exposure to wind, can create variations of as much as two zones either way.

US Department of Agriculture Hardiness Zones

(These zones are based on the average annual minimum temperature for each zone)

Zone 1	Below –50° F
Zone 2	–50° to –40°
Zone 3	–40° to –30°
Zone 4	–30° to –20°
Zone 5	–20° to –10°
Zone 6	–10° to 0°
Zone 7	0° to 10°
Zone 8	10° to 20°
Zone 9	20° to 30°
Zone 10	30° to 40°
Zone 11	Above 40°

Pieris formosa forrestii **'Wakehurst'** is a superb evergreen, both in flower and in spring growth.

Beyond the practical aspects of growing shrubs there are the stories which make them 'come alive'. These concern their origins, wild or otherwise, their discovery and introduction to gardens and the people responsible. These people include plant hunters, missionaries, sea captains and adventurers, as well as rich and influential patrons, nurserymen, gardeners, plant breeders and all those of a curious mind, with sharp eyes or skilled hands. From such sources have our gardens developed and all who make or enjoy a garden owe them a debt of gratitude. Wherever possible, therefore, I have given at least brief details of how and when the shrubs in this book originated, their awards from the Royal Horticultural Society as well as their date of introduction to cultivation or commerce.

The origin and pronunciation of the names

For gardeners, especially first-timers, one of the greatest deterrents to using botanical names is their correct pronunciation. To help readers understand and pronounce the names of shrubs featured in this book I have given against each main entry a short explanation. These are based on examples contained in Allen J Coombes' excellent pocket guide *The Collingridge Dictionary of Plant Names.*

SPRING

Spring is the most exciting and the most exhausting season in the garden. Exciting, because of the emergence of new shoots and leaves and the appearance of countless flowers. Exhausting, because flowers appear in such numbers and at such a pace that the mind can hardly cope with it. So anxious are they to flower in spring that shrubs almost fall over themselves like vegetable lemmings, one following upon another in rapid succession. For those of us who have planted shrubs the previous autumn, spring finds us entering the garden with fingers crossed hoping to see those first tell-tale signs of life, confirmation that our efforts have not been in vain.

Berberis 'Goldilocks'

Berberis are not everyone's cup of tea, especially large berberis. An exception is generally made, however, in the case of *Berberis darwinii* whose dark spine-toothed evergreen leaves prove such an effective backing for the drooping clusters of orange or orange-yellow flowers in mid to late spring. Even when the flowers fade there is more to come in the shape of pea-sized berries of plum purple with a blue-grey bloom. It is a native of Chile and was first discovered in 1835 by Charles Darwin (after whom it is named) during his time as naturalist on the famous voyage of HMS *Beagle*. It was introduced 14 years later from the island of Chiloe by William Lobb, a Cornish plant hunter employed by the Exeter firm of Veitch.

It is a hardy, handsome shrub of compact rounded or dome-shaped habit capable of reaching 3–6m (10–12ft) high and as much across in a sheltered situation (even more in mild districts) and has long been popular as a hedge. It is at its most impressive, however, as a single specimen or as a close planted group of between three and five in a large lawn, where it can be admired from all angles. Commonly cultivated and easy to propagate from seed or from cuttings in late summer, it is one of the most easily recognised of a notoriously difficult group of plants.

Not so common or so easy to multiply is *Berberis valdiviana*, a noble evergreen shrub, taller, to 5m (16ft), than the last and quite unlike it in leaf and aspect. The habit of *B. valdiviana* is more upright with stout shoots and branches clothed with large, dark glossy green leaves up to 7.5cm (3in) long which at most are armed with a few spiny teeth, more commonly without. Indeed, some people take it to be some kind of holly and as there are several smooth-leaved cultivars of *Ilex aquifolium* the comparison is understandable. On closer examination, however, the strongly spined shoots give the game away though even these are occasionally spineless.

It is at its best in late spring when the branches are draped with dense clusters of small cup-shaped flowers which are a characteristic saffron yellow, quite unlike other berberis species I know. These are sometimes followed by small rounded purple berries with a blue-grey bloom but their appearance is not reliable in our climate. Denied its berries the propagator must rely on cuttings to increase this species but even here he is challenged by a great reluctance on the part of cuttings to root, hence the scarcity of this shrub in cultivation. Many plants offered in the trade have been grafted onto the deciduous *Berberis thunbergii*. Indeed, when I worked for the Winchester nursery firm of Hilliers in the 1960s and 1970s we kept a TAS (To Await Supply) book containing the names of all those difficult to supply plants together with the names of customers who wanted them. *B. valdiviana* never left this book and its list of admirers was as long as my arm. It is not hard to understand why this species attracts such attention especially if you stand as I did recently in an Irish garden by a 4.5m (15ft) specimen covered with flower and humming with bees.

Berberis
(**Family:** Berberidaceae)
Pronunciation: *ber*-be-ris
Meaning: the Arabic name.

Previous pages: *Corylopsis pauciflora*, an excellent shrub for small gardens; *Camellia × williamsii* **'J.C. Williams'**, one of the first of its kind.

As a wild plant, *B. valdiviana* is native to Chile, from Chillan to Valdivia province and was first described from the latter in 1856 hence the name. It was first introduced to cultivation in 1902 but the present stock in our gardens owes its introduction to Clarence Elliot (father of Joe Elliot, the alpine plant specialist) and Dr Balfour-Gourlay, who collected seed from near Temuco in Chile in 1929. Although it has been known to suffer damage in severe winters it is generally regarded as hardy and is happy in the average garden soil, limy or otherwise.

Imagine now, a berberis as spectacular as *B. valdiviana* but as easy to propagate and grow as *B. darwinii*. The idea of such a hybrid intrigued for a long time Peter Dummer, Master Propagator at Hilliers Nurseries in Hampshire. Peter has produced many hybrids in his time but this he considered one of his greatest challenges. The cross was made in 1978 using a good form of *B. darwinii* as the pollen parent. The following year two seeds from the cross were sown and one of the resulting seedlings grew strongly to flower for the first time in 1984. Named 'Goldilocks', the hybrid is intermediate in character between the parents, the viciously spiny shoots to 3.5m (12ft) or more with both smooth and spine-toothed leaves larger than those of *B. darwinii*. The flowers, freely borne in mid to late spring, are larger individually than those of *B. valdiviana* and darker in colour, the influence of *B. darwinii* being quite clear. Being an F1 hybrid, 'Goldilocks' shows great vigour and, more importantly, roots easily from cuttings in late summer.

Berberis 'Goldilocks'
- HARDY
- FULL SUN
- MOST SOILS
- EVERGREEN
- ZONES 5–8

Camellia japonica 'Midnight Serenade'

In the garden of a large stone built house near my childhood home in Bolton, Lancashire, there once grew a camellia. Although it was planted against the sunny wall of the house and had reached a substantial size it rarely flowered and when it did the red flowers were small and not freely borne. It was, nevertheless, a sight for sore eyes and at that time the only camellia I knew of which was growing out of doors. Camellias were grown under glass, of course, in the central parks nursery, pampered and preened, their leaves periodically brushed with a nicotine wash to kill scale insects or wiped with a Volk-soaked rag to improve their natural gloss. But these could not begin to compete with the colourful crotons (Codiaeums) and other tender foliage exotics whose company they shared.

It was not until I began to travel and visit gardens in other areas that I came to realise how hardy the common camellia really was and, furthermore, what a great number of cultivars existed in cultivation. *Camellia japonica*, in one form or another, is the most commonly grown of its clan. It is generally easily identified by its dense almost solid bushy habit and its bold often broad or rounded evergreen leaves which are dark almost black green and glossy above. The flowers may be cup-shaped and single, semi-double or double with several variations such as peony form, anemone form, etc. Colour, too, varies from palest pink to red and white while some flowers are variegated, striped or blotched pink, red or white. There are endless variations.

In the wild, *C. japonica* is native to Japan on the islands of Honshu, Shikoku and Kyushu where it grows in coastal areas, sometimes amongst scrub at sea-level. It is also found wild in Korea, the Lin Kin Islands and in China. Wild *C. japonica* generally has pinkish red flowers opening from late winter to early summer, depending on altitude, and can reach small tree size, 9m (30ft), after many years. It has been cultivated in Japan for centuries and is found in the gardens of temples and shrines there in great numbers and variety. Its first introduction to Europe, according to some evidence, took place accidentally about the beginning of the eighteenth century; living plants being brought to England aboard a ship of the East India Company.

One story has it that the Company had intended bringing home the tea plant (*Camellia sinensis*) in order to establish it in their Indian and American estates and thereby cut out the Chinese profit, but Chinese officials were either wise to the situation or else made a genuine mistake and substituted the tea plants with the more ornamental but economically useless *C. japonica*. Other introductions were made to Europe during the eighteenth century and by the middle of the nineteenth many hundreds of new cultivars had been raised in England and Europe. It continued as a popular greenhouse ornamental until the turn of the present century when it began to lose favour. Then came the First World War and due to the absence of many gardeners on active service, greenhouses and conservatories housing camellias fell into disrepair while elsewhere camellias were planted outside to save time spent on watering and other operations.

For the first time in many gardens and estates camellias were having to live with the elements and to many people's surprise most of them coped admirably. Since then *C. japonica*, certainly, has been regarded quite rightly as a hardy evergreen and, given certain conditions, will thrive outside in all but the coldest inland areas. The main conditions conducive to good health and performance are first and foremost a neutral to slightly acid soil, preferably one cool and moist but well drained and furnished with plenty of humus. They enjoy also an annual mulching of organic matter especially leaf mould, so long as it is acid not alkaline in reaction, e.g. oak rather than beech.

Those living in chalk country or elsewhere with an alkaline soil might consider growing camellias in large containers or in raised beds filled with an acid or ericaceous compost. Camellias also like shelter from cold winds or draughts. This can be provided by a wall or hedge or by other, tougher shrubs. In cooler areas, they need sun and warmth to encourage flowering but given that their flowers when subjected to frost turn brown on exposure to the early morning sun, they are best planted against a wall that is sunny in the late morning and afternoon only. Alternatively, if tree cover or the position of a building of some sort prevents the early morning sun from falling on the flowers any sunny wall is ideal. In many

Camellia japonica
'Midnight Serenade'
- HARDY
- SUN OR HALF-SHADE
- LIME-FREE SOILS
- EVERGREEN
- ZONES 7–9

Camellia japonica
(**Family:** Theaceae)
Pronunciation: ka-*mel*-lee-a
Meaning: after George Joseph Kamel (Camellus) (1661–1706), pharmacist who studied the Philippines flora
Pronunciation: ja-*pon*-i-ka
Meaning: of Japan.

areas *C. japonica* can be seen thriving in light woodland cover, their flowers often at their best before the leaves of deciduous trees have expanded. Filtered sunlight or half-shade is the key factor not dense shade. Also, when planting among trees avoid putting them too near the trunks or where tree roots are close to the surface. As a rule of thumb, the colder the area in which camellias are grown the more sun and warmth they require to flower.

Apart from frost damage to blooms, camellias have few problems when grown in good conditions outside and, curiously, they seem immune to the presence of honey fungus even when rhododendrons and other shrubs in the vicinity are suffering. Of other problems, virus and bud drop are the most common. Some cultivars of *C. japonica* have yellow mottling on their leaves most of which is genetic in nature and, though unsightly, does not affect the vigour of the plant. Flower-buds being shed before opening can have several causes; faulty cultivation, excess water from bad drainage, soil too dry especially during droughts, or sudden changes in temperature. In addition, some camellias naturally shed buds when too many are produced on the same stem.

Of the many hundreds of cultivars of *C. japonica* that have been named over the years only a comparatively small selection are seen outside the collections of specialists or the famous gardens like Exbury in Hampshire and those in Windsor Great Park. A good number are available from specialist growers, however, and I shall discuss here just a few of those which have proved themselves in cultivation. The majority are of medium to large size 2–3m (6–10ft) eventually, and as much across, flowering in most areas from late winter through spring.

Starting with the reds there are few to match 'Adolphe Audusson', a justifiably popular mid season camellia raised in France by M. Audusson of Angers in 1877. It is of medium compact growth producing large semi-double flowers of blood red with conspicuous yellow anthered stamens. It received an Award of Merit from the Royal Horticultural Society in 1934 and a First Class Certificate in 1956.

'Donckelaarii' is another mid-season flowerer and considering that it has been around since 1834 at least, the year it was introduced from China to Belgium, it says a lot for its garden worthiness. It is named after M. Donckelaar, Director of the Royal Gardens at Ghent, early last century and is a slow-growing bushy camellia with large semi-double flowers of pure red, marbled white. It received an Award of Merit from the RHS in 1960.

'Apollo' is another fine camellia, this time of vigorous open growth with semi-double rose-red flowers occasionally blotched white. It was raised by the English nurseryman William Paul of Cheshunt and Waltham Cross, Hertfordshire in about 1900 and received an Award of Merit from the RHS in 1956. A more recent introduction is 'Midnight Serenade'. Raised at the famous camellia nurseries of Nuccio in California in 1973, this shrub is a superb single mid to late season camellia with medium to large flowers of a brilliant dark red with irregular twisted petals and a sheef of gold-tipped stamens.

Among the pink and rose-pink cultivars 'Elegans' is still regarded as one of the very best. Raised in England by Chandler's nursery of Vauxhall in 1831 and sometimes found listed in old catalogues as 'Chandleri Elegans' it is of slow spreading growth producing large, sometimes very large, anemone-form flowers which are rose-pink, the central petaloids often spotted white. It was given an Award of Merit by the RHS in 1953 and a First Class Certificate in 1958.

'Debutante' is an American cultivar released by the Magnolia Gardens of South Carolina early this century. It is a camellia of vigorous upright habit with clear, light pink peony-form flowers (mid to late season). 'Contessa Lavinia Maggi' was raised in Italy during the last century. The large formal double-flowers are pale pink or white with broad rose-cerise stripes. 'Lady Vansittart' is similarly bi-coloured, white striped rose-pink, but the flowers are of semi-double form with wavy edged petals. The leaves are also wavy edged. This is a slow-growing cultivar. Regarded as one of the best of the bi-colours is 'Betty Sheffield Supreme', a camellia of compact growth with large loose informal double-flowers of white with each slightly wavy petal edged pink to rose-red in picotee style. It was introduced by Mrs G.W. Alday of Thomasville, Georgia in 1960.

White-flowered cultivars of *C. japonica* are so easily bruised that they are not so popular in British gardens as pink and red ones. 'Elegans Champagne' is a descendant of 'Elegans' and is similar in growth and flower form but in colour a waxy white with feathered outer petals and a central dome of creamy petaloids. Quite different is 'Alba Simplex' the most reliable, but with large white single flowers and conspicuous yellow antlers. It received an Award of Merit from the RHS in 1948. One of the oldest of all, and still one of the best of its kind, is 'Alba Plena' which was introduced to England from China by Captain Connor of the East India Company in 1792, the first double camellia to reach the West. It is a camellia of great antiquity and is said to be recognisable in Chinese manuscripts as far back as the Song Dynasty (AD960–1280). It is slow and erect in growth producing white formal double-flowers of medium size early in the season. It received an Award of Merit from the RHS in 1948.

All these camellias can be propagated by cuttings in late summer. When necessary, camellias can be pruned to prevent an untidy habit, even hard pruning will be tolerated to re-shape or rejuvenate a specimen. This is best carried out in late spring after flowering.

Camellia × williamsii 'Bow Bells'

Caerhays, near Gorran on the south coast of Cornwall, is one of the finest woodland gardens in Britain. More of a collection than a garden in the normally accepted sense, it is situated on a steep slope facing south over the castellated roofs of the Victorian house and home of the Williams family. The oldest trees are oak and beech and there is a rich native ground-cover in places best seen in spring when primroses, violets and wood anemones create colourful carpets of yellow, purple and white.

The main attraction, however, for plantsmen certainly, is the rich assemblage of exotic trees and shrubs which have found in these woods a home from home. The Chinese collections of George Forrest and E.H. Wilson are well represented here, especially rhododendrons, magnolias and camellias. The man responsible for the original planting was J.C. Williams whose son Julian and grandson Charles together, with their long-serving head gardener Philip Tregunna, are continuing the good work.

One of the many introductions raised from Forrest's seed at Caerhays was *Camellia saluenensis*, a native of Yunnan in south-west China where it grows in hillside scrub and on woodland margins. Caerhays already had a good collection of *Camellia japonica* cultivars when seed of *C. saluenensis* was received in 1924 and the new arrival was soon growing happily in the woodland. From a garden point of view, *C. saluenensis* differs from *C. japonica* in its more open habit with relatively narrow finely toothed leaves lacking the high polish of the other, while the pale blush pink to deep rose flowers are more tubular bell-shaped and more freely borne. J.C. Williams, quickly recognising the potential of crossing the last named with selected cultivars of *C. japonica*, wasted no time and during the 1930s and 1940s several selected seedlings from these hybrids were named and introduced to commerce.

Around the same time, similar crosses were being carried out by another great gardener, Colonel Stephenson Clarke, at Borde Hill near Haywards Heath in Sussex. Since then, many more cultivars have been produced from this cross in Britain and other countries, especially Australia and New Zealand. The Williamsii camellias, as they are generally referred to, are superb late winter to spring flowering evergreens for medium-sized or large gardens, although some being less vigorous are suitable for smaller gardens too. On the whole, they tend towards a loosely branched, spreading habit 3–5m (10–16ft) high and as much or more across eventually. Their finely toothed leaves are generally neater and more slender pointed giving the plant a more informal, less solid appearance than *C. japonica*.

Flowers vary from single tubular bell-shaped to large semi-doubles and doubles, their collective weight in some cultivars causing the long branches to bend. Another characteristic, important from a garden point of view, concerns the mature flowers which when shed form a colourful carpet on the ground, while those of *C. japonica* and its cultivars usually remain on the branches until after maturity, their browned petals providing an untidy aftermath.

As for growing conditions, the Williamsii camellias have the same likes and dislikes as *C. japonica* but it must be said that they flower better in a more open, especially sunnier, site and are more tolerant of exposure although preferring shelter, of course. They have proved more reliable in British cultivation than *C. japonica* and many cultivars flourish in some of Britain's colder and more northerly areas, their flower buds initiated by lower temperatures than those required by the other.

Camellia × williamsii
'Bow Bells'

- HARDY
- SUN OR HALF-SHADE
- LIME-FREE SOILS
- EVERGREEN
- ZONES 7–9

Propagation and pruning are the same as for *C. japonica*. Well furnished camellias in flower provide excellent cut material for indoor decoration and (double-flowered cultivars especially) the most exotic, if outsize, buttonholes.

Here is a selection of some of my favourite Williamsii camellias suitable for general cultivation. The single flowered ones must include 'St Ewe', one of J.C. Williams' seedlings named after a village near Caerhays. Introduced to commerce in 1947, its flowers are funnel-shaped of a lovely phlox pink, opening over a long period. Its habit is tall and bushy and it was recognised by the RHS in 1974 when it was awarded a First Class Certificate after Trial at Wisley.

In 'November Pink' the flowers are larger and rose-madder, beginning to open before Christmas in milder areas and continuing until late spring. It was given an Award of Merit by the RHS in December 1950. J.C. Williams itself was the first seedling at Caerhays to be named in 1940. Its flowers open flat and are produced over a long period. In colour they are a light dog–rose pink with darker shadings. It received an Award of Merit after Trial at Wisley in 1977.

In 'Bow Bells' the flowers are semi-double, of a bright rose and produced continuously over a long period. It is one of the best of its kind for general cultivation.

'Jenefer Carlyon' has semi-double clear silvery pink flowers and a bushy habit. It was raised by the late Miss Gillian Carlyon of Tregrehan, Cornwall in 1962 and received an Award of Merit from the RHS in 1984. Its raiser received the Reginald Cory Memorial Cup for the best hardy deliberate hybrid shown that year.

'Donation' is one of the most popular camellia hybrids ever raised and can be seen flourishing in many gardens. Its habit is vigorous and erect, producing through much of spring large semi-double orchid pink flowers. So profusely borne are they on an established plant that the branches arch under their weight. It was raised by Colonel Stephenson Clarke at Borde Hill, Sussex in the 1930s and first exhibited at a RHS Show in 1941 when it received an Award of Merit, to be followed in 1974 by a First Class Certificate after Trial at Wisley. The *C. japonica* parent Col. Clarke used was 'Donckelaarii'. 'Donation' was the favourite camellia of the late Jack Brice, first Head Gardener of the Hillier Gardens and Arboretum near Romsey in Hampshire. He was one of the last of the 'old school' head gardeners who began as a garden boy and progressed through the ranks eventually to manage one of the largest and most famous plant collections of its kind in the temperate regions. His practical knowledge of plants and their cultivation was enormous and he was a credit to his profession.

Similar to 'Donation', but considered superior by some enthusiasts, is 'Brigadoon' which was raised by the Armstrong Nursery of California in 1960. This has rose-pink, medium, semi-double flowers. From L. Jury in New Zealand, meanwhile, we have two fine camellias in 'Anticipation' and Debbie'. The first of these is of narrow habit bearing large rose-crimson flowers of peony form up to 10cm (5in) across. It received a First Class Certificate after Trial at Wisley in 1974. 'Debbie' is also rather upright, producing peony-

Camellia × williamsii
(**Family:** Theaceae)
Pronunciation: ka-*mel*-lee-a
Meaning: after George Joseph Kamel (Camellus) (1661–1706), pharmacist who studied the Philippines flora
Pronunciation: wil-*yămz*-ee-ee
Meaning: after J.C. Williams of Caerhays, Cornwall who raised many forms of this hybrid.

form rose-pink flowers over a long period. It makes the perfect large buttonhole and regularly causes comment in my garden when in flower. 'Waterlily' is another New Zealander whose flowers are a formal double with a raised centre and light pink shaded lavender pink petals which are inrolled at the margin. One of the best of the reds is 'Freedom Bell', raised by the Nuccio Nurseries of California and introduced to commerce in 1965. The flowers are small to medium sized, semi-double of 'hose-in-hose' form (one flower within another) and coral red. Its upright compact habit is ideally suited to smaller gardens.

In addition to the above Williamsii camellias there are several other lovely hybrids worth considering for more sheltered gardens where, in late winter or early spring they produce a stunning display, especially after a warm summer. Most notable are those with *Camellia reticulata* and *Camellia saluenensis* as parents. The former is an impressive tree species from Yunnan in south-west China which has been cultivated for centuries in that province and is represented there in temple and monastery gardens and courtyards by a rich variety of cultivars most of which, however, are too tender for outdoor cultivation in all but the mildest of areas.

Hybrids to go for include 'Inspiration' which has large semi-double flowers not unlike those of 'Donation' but which are more weatherproof and darker in colour. It was raised at Exbury Gardens in Hampshire and introduced to commerce in 1954. It is a free-growing shrub to 3m (10ft) or more eventually and it received an Award of Merit from the RHS in 1984. From the same source comes 'Inamorata' with rich rose-pink single flowers and a bold stack of yellow anthered stamens. It was introduced in 1950 and is a cross between *C. saluenensis* and the wild form of *C. reticulata* introduced by George Forrest from Yunnan in 1924. 'Leonard Messel' was raised at Nymans Gardens, Handcross, Sussex and named after the late owner by his wife. Introduced to commerce in 1958, it is of vigorous habit with large semi-double rose-pink flowers with wavy petals and a bold boss of yellow stamens. It is a cross between the wild *C. reticulata* and *Camellia* × *williamsii* 'Mary Christian'.

Very different in every way is *C.* 'Cornish Snow' a free-growing Saluenensis hybrid of elegant habit to 3m (10ft) or more with small slender pointed leaves inherited from the other parent *Camellia cuspidata*. The small white single flowers with golden anthers are freely borne along the arching branches and a large bush at its best is a lovely sight. It was raised by J.C. Williams at Caerhays in about 1930 receiving an Award of Merit from the RHS in 1948. A charming variation of this hybrid is Cornish Snow 'Winton', named and introduced to commerce by Hilliers Nurseries in 1948. It differs in the colour of its flowers which are a pale almond pink. Both are suitable for a sunny or lightly shaded site sheltered from cold winds. Similarly neat in habit is 'Spring Festival', a seedling of *C. cuspidata* introduced to commerce by Toicho Domoto of California in 1975. The small, soft pink flowers are rose-form double and are quite exquisite. As the habit is fairly upright, it is suitable for the smaller garden, with coppery-red young leaves as an added bonus.

Ceanothus arboreus 'Trewithen Blue'

Ceanothus arboreus
'Trewithen Blue'

- FAIRLY HARDY
- SUN
- MOST WELL-DRAINED SOILS
- EVERGREEN
- ZONES 8–10

Although they belong to different families and are as alike as chalk and cheese, *Lyonothamnus floribundus* and *Ceanothus arboreus* have one thing in common and that is they both hail from the islands off the coast of California which include Santa Cruz and Santa Catalina. To the best of my knowledge these are the only plants in British cultivation endemic to these islands. This means they are found nowhere else in the wild. Interesting then that despite their most favoured abode, they should deign to grow with us.

Lyonothamnus, admittedly, is mainly grown in the milder areas of Britain and Ireland especially in the south and west but *Ceanothus arboreus* is much tougher, although I would not recommend it for cold inland areas, while a severe winter will damage, if not kill it even in the more favoured gardens. It is, nevertheless, one of the hardiest and most reliable of its genus, suitable for large- or medium-sized gardens where it is best accommodated against a large wall or similar support. Naturally, given its native climate, it thrives best in full sun and a well-drained soil, acid or alkaline.

It is one of the largest *Ceanothus* species, capable of 6m (20ft) or more against a wall, and of similar spread. The evergreen leaves, too, are large, up to 10cm (4in) long, bright green above, pale grey felted beneath. The pale blue flowers are individually tiny but are borne in large dense conical clusters (panicles) in spring, earlier in a mild winter or in a warm protected corner. It commonly produces flowers off and on throughout summer but these are nothing in comparison with the spring display.

Even better is the cultivar 'Trewithen Blue' with flowers of a deeper blue and slightly scented. It is the most commonly planted form of *C. arboreus* in Britain today and one of the most successful of all ceanothus for British gardens. Given its great vigour it is a shrub which may need controlling in mild areas especially when trained against a wall. This can be achieved by pruning back or shortening the flowering shoots immediately after the flowers have faded. In a mild or Mediterranean climate the flowers are produced almost continuously and such is its vigour, it is one of the most reliable and satisfactory flowering evergreens for filling a large space.

Its name refers to Trewithen Gardens at Grampound Road near Truro in Cornwall where this plant was received as an unnamed seedling from the USA in the early 1950s. It was then being grown simply as *C. arboreus* but some years later it was seen by Neil Treseder, proprietor of the now defunct Treseder's nursery of Truro who suggested the cultivar name. He was also the first to propagate this shrub, introducing it to commerce in about 1960.

Propagation is by cuttings in late summer and it is worth having a young plant or two in reserve just in case a hard winter puts paid to your old one. 'Trewithen Blue' received an Award of Merit from the Royal Horticultural Society in 1967.

There are several other evergreen spring flowering ceanothus worth considering for a sunny border or wall in the garden. They include 'Delight' (rich blue flowers), 'Italian Skies' (deep blue), 'Southmead' (bright blue) and × *veitchianus* (bright deep blue). The last named is one of the hardiest and most satisfactory of the smaller leaved hybrids for general cultivation.

Ceanothus arboreus
(**Family:** Rhamnaceae)
Pronunciation: kee-a-*nō*-thus but usually pronounced *see*-a-nō-thus
Meaning: Greek name for a spiny shrub
Pronunciation: ar-*bo*-ree-us
Meaning: tree-like.

Choisya 'Aztec Pearl'

In 1989 the Hampshire nursery firm of Hilliers celebrated its 125th anniversary with the launching of the first recorded hybrid *Choisya* 'Aztec Pearl'. A deliberate hybrid, it was made by Peter Moore, one of an elite group of Hillier propagators whose skill and enthusiasm over many years have produced some of the best of that firm's introductions. The Choisya story began in the 1970s when the late Sir Harold Hillier received from a friend in Georgia, USA, plants of *Choisya arizonica* (now regarded as *Choisya dumosa* var. *arizonica*), a native of southern Arizona where it grows in desert and dry oak woodland in Pima, Graham and Cochise counties. It was first discovered in 1884 growing on limestone ledges over 1,300m (4,000ft) up in the Santa Rita Mountains. This is a much smaller shrub than the familiar Mexican orange *Choisya ternata*, with slender stems and branches and leaves with three to six (mainly five) thread-like, toothed leaflets. Both leaf stalks and shoots are hairy and warty while the scented flowers which appear in late spring are carried singly on slender stalks. These are white or blush tinted.

A plant was grown in the Hillier Arboretum but after flourishing for a few years it perished. Cuttings had been taken, however, and the plants were grown under glass to encourage good growth. In 1982, Peter Moore decided to attempt a cross between this plant and *C. ternata*. The cross was made both ways but although seed capsules formed in each case only those borne on the *C. ternata* mother plant produced viable seeds, two in number. These were sown the following year (at the end of winter), germination taking three weeks and by autumn both seedlings were already 25cm (10in) high and bushy. Their first winter was spent in a cool greenhouse being potted on and grown outside the following summer. By the second autumn, flower-buds had formed and despite spending that winter in tubs outside, they remained healthy, despite snow and low temperatures.

In May 1985, three years after the cross was initiated, the hybrids flowered and Peter was delighted with the results. One of the seedlings had larger flowers than the other and it is this which was eventually given the name 'Aztec Pearl' a reference to the Mexican home of *C. ternata* and the skilled Aztec craftsmen who flourished 1,000 years ago creating intricate carvings and adornments, often encrusted with elaborate, feathery motifs of pearls and jewels. 'Aztec Pearl' was officially launched at the 1989 Chelsea Flower Show. It is a relatively small bushy shrub probably 1–1.3m (3–4ft) high and as much or more across eventually, with minutely warty shoots and short stalked leaves divided into three to five finger-like leaflets.

The flowers in late spring are pink in bud opening white with yellow anthers, the pink often retained on the backs of the petals when first opened. They are larger than those of *C. ternata*, 4cm (1 1/2in) across, and sweetly fragrant borne singly or in threes from the upper leaf axils at the ends of the previous year's shoots.

'Aztec Pearl' is proving a most attractive evergreen, bolder and hardier than *C. dumosa* var. *arizonica*, smaller, more elegant in foliage and with larger flowers than *C. ternata*. It enjoys similar growing conditions to the last named and appears to be at least of equal hardiness. It is also, given its size, more suitable for the sheltered terrace or courtyard, although, it does not challenge it for the larger garden. It may be propagated by cuttings in late summer.

Choisya
(**Family:** Rutaceae)
Pronunciation: *shwūz*-ee-a but usually pronounced *choy*-zee-a
Meaning: after Jacques Denis Choisy (1799–1859), Swiss botanist.

Choisya ternata

Known as the Mexican Orange *Choisya ternata* is one of the very few Mexican plants which can be regarded as successful in cool temperate gardens. It is not quite in the vanguard of hardy plants and will not thrive in cold, exposed situations especially in the north, nor is it immune to defoliation or die-back during severe weather

Above: *Choisya* 'Aztec Pearl'

- HARDY, BUT PREFERS SHELTER FROM WIND
- SUN
- MOST WELL-DRAINED SOILS
- EVERGREEN
- ZONES 8–9

Choisya ternata

- HARDY, BUT BEST IN SHELTERED SITE
- SUN OR HALF-SHADE
- MOST WELL-DRAINED SOILS
- EVERGREEN
- ZONES 8–9

elsewhere. It is sometimes the case with choisyas grown in a rich soil that soft growth suffers most from spring frosts even after colder winter temperatures have had no effect. One way of preventing this is to provide a sheltered position and a not too rich soil to encourage shorter 'harder' growth. By and large, however, it is a shrub worth trying in most gardens, space permitting. Not surprisingly, given its country of origin, it enjoys sun and warmth but is remarkably tolerant of shade which makes it such a good plant for town and city gardens. In areas enjoying regularly warm summers such as the Mediterranean it grows best away from the full glare of the sun.

Resentful of disturbance, *C. ternata* is normally container-grown by nurserymen but even small plants once established grow vigorously, forming in time a compact mound of glistening dark evergreen foliage, anything from 2–3m (6–10ft) high and as much or more across. The leaves comprise three leathery leaflets which have almost a lacquered appearance above and are pungently scented when bruised or crushed. Hold them to the light and you will see they are dotted with numerous translucent oil glands.

The white flowers 2.5–3cm (1-1¹/4in) across appear in crowded clusters from the upper leaf axils in mid to late spring though odd clusters are likely to appear at almost any other time, even in winter, should the weather be mild. If for no other reason, *C. ternata* is worth growing for its foliage and flower but those who place great store on scent, value this shrub for the sweet fragrance of its flowers which are deliciously scented of hawthorn.

Given a well-drained soil it cares not whether it be acid or alkaline in reaction and providing it is sheltered from cold winds or draughts seems amenable to most garden situations. It is ideal for cutting for the home and will even take hard pruning should this be necessary to control growth. This is best done after flowering in early summer.

In its native Mexico, *C. ternata* is more familiar in gardens, where it has been grown for centuries, than in the wild where it is rare and only found in a few locations in San Louis Potosi and Toluca. It was first introduced to European cultivation in 1825 and was awarded a First Class Certificate by the Royal Horticultural Society as long ago as 1880. Surprisingly, considering the length of time it has been in cultivation and its popularity among gardeners, *C. ternata* has produced no cultivars, none that is until 1978, when a tiny variegated sport was found on a bush in Hampshire by Peter Catt, founder of Liss Forest Nursery, Greatham near Petersfield in Hampshire. According to Peter, the original cutting he made had leaflets with a white edge but subsequently it produced a shoot with golden leaves. Slowly, stock was built up until Peter decided to place it with a firm specialising in micro-propagation. Early results produced both green and gold leaved plants but eventually this problem was resolved and in 1986 Peter's golden choisya was duly launched at the Chelsea Flower Show under the cultivar name 'Sundance'.

It has since become widely grown and is valued for its mounds of bright yellow young foliage which pales to yellow-green then green as it matures. The leaves in winter are yellow concealing or overlying the yellow-green or discoloured older leaves. Flowers are produced as in the typical green leaved plant but not so freely (if at all on young specimens). As a year round golden leaved evergreen, 'Sundance' is undoubtedly at its best in spring and early summer but is useful in winter especially when grown against a dark background or with dark leaved evergreens such as skimmias. It also makes an impressive specimen plant for the large terrace either in a bed or in a large container. Like the type, it is liable to damage in severe winters and is specially deserving of shelter and protection when low temperatures are forecast. Both *C. ternata* and 'Sundance' can be propagated by cuttings in late summer or by layering.

Choisya ternata
(**Family:** Rutaceae)
Pronunciation: *shwūz*-ee-a usually pronounced *choy*-zee-a
Meaning: after Jacques Denis Choisy (1799–1859), Swiss botanist
Pronunciation: ter-*nah*-ta
Meaning: in threes (the leaflets).

Corylopsis veitchiana

Corylopsis veitchiana
- HARDY, BUT PREFERS SHELTER FROM SPRING FROSTS
- SUN OR HALF-SHADE
- LIME-FREE SOILS
- ZONES 6-8

Among the several corylopsis presently in cultivation Corylopsis veitchiana is, in my opinion, one of the most distinct and ornamental. It is a large deciduous shrub of strong upright growth especially when young, broadening later and reaching eventually 2.4m (8ft), more in a sheltered site, and as much if not more across. The bristle-toothed leaves are a rich green in colour, purplish when very young and up to 10cm (5in) long with almost parallel sides, a characteristic feature. These emerge in late spring normally just after the flowers and turn yellow before falling in autumn. The individual flowers are small, cup-shaped and primrose yellow with protruding brick-red anthers which pale on ripening. They are carried in close packed, pendulous clusters 5–7cm (2–2$^{1}/_{2}$in) long, draping the previous year's shoots.

The second name *veitchiana* commemorates the firm of James Veitch and Sons in whose nursery at Coombe Wood, Surrey, plants were first raised. It was introduced to cultivation in 1900 by E.H. Wilson who found the shrub fairly common in western

Hubei province, in China, in thickets and on woodland margins. He considered this species sufficiently meritorious to include it in his book *Aristocrats of the Garden* and I fully agree with his assessment despite the fact that, in common with other corylopsis, its flowers and emerging leaves are subject to damage by late frosts. During my 18 years at the Hillier Arboretum *C. veitchiana* suffered this fate on only three occasions and each time made a full recovery. It is prudent, however, to plant it in a position sheltered by other shrubs or in light woodland.

It is also worth bearing in mind that the effect of flowering is considerably enhanced when seen against a dark background such as that provided by evergreens. Apart from the frost problem, only one cloud compromises this shrub's further advance in cultivation and it concerns the name. Indeed, here is a classic example of what many gardeners regard as 'botanists spoiling a good thing'. According to recent expert opinion, *C. veitchiana* is not sufficiently distinct to be regarded as a species in its own right and has been removed to another species – *C. wilsonii* – not even as a variety I might add but as a mere form! If you wish to be seen as 'running with the botanical pack' you will in future refer to this shrub as *Corylopsis sinensis* variety *calvescens* forma *veitchiana*. Poor old Veitch, he must be thundering in his heavenly nursery but at least the authorities responsible stopped short of sinking his species altogether. One of the problems when a species is demoted in this way and its full name increases as a result, is that people new to gardening tend to be put off; 'what a mouthful' they say as they pass on to something less indigestible. Those who know *C. veitchiana* will doubtless continue with the old name. Propagation is by cuttings in summer.

Corylopsis veitchiana
(**Family:** Hamamelidaceae)
Pronunciation: ko-ril-*op*-sis
Meaning: from *Corylus* and Greek-*opsis* indicating resemblance, (the habit and leaves are similar to *Corylus*)
Pronunciation: veech-ee-*ah*-na
Meaning: after the Veitch nursery.

Cytisus scoparius maritimus

Anyone familiar with the Channel Islands or the coast of West Cornwall may have seen a low prostrate shrub forming curtains of green angular stems on the cliffs above the sea. These curtains can be quite sizeable if the shrub is long established and they are easy to spot from the beach below. Visit these cliffs in May and you will see them plastered with bold yellow pea-flowers staining the rocks and banks from a distance. It is a distinct and localised form of our Common broom or Whin, known as *Cytisus scoparius* ssp. *maritimus* and it is also found in similar places in Pembrokeshire, on Lundy and in West Cork. When it was first taken into cultivation is not recorded but it is available from several nursery sources usually under the synonym *C. scoparius prostratus*.

I first saw it on the famous limestone rock garden in the University Botanic Garden, Cambridge where it grew on a raised area, its stems blanketing the ground for 2m (6ft) before tumbling down a rockface. Later, we planted it on a dry wall top in the Hillier Arboretum and here too its sheets of bloom in late spring always attracted attention.

Cytisus scoparius* ssp. *maritimus
(**Family:** Leguminosae)
Pronunciation: *si*-ti-sus
Meaning: from *kytisos*, Greek name for these or similar shrubs
Pronunciation: skō-*pah*-ree-us
Meaning: broom-like
Pronunciation: ma-*ri*-ti-mus
Meaning: growing near the sea.

Cytisus scoparius maritimus
- HARDY
- SUN
- LIME-FREE SOILS
- ZONES 6–8

Like the common kind, it is quite hardy and easy in cultivation preferring, however, a lime-free soil and a sunny situation. Interestingly, it comes true from seed, otherwise it is easily propagated by semi-ripened cuttings in late summer.

There are available many lovely brooms, mostly seedlings or hybrids of *C. scoparius*, which are well worth considering for gardens on lime-free soils. They include, 'Boskoop Ruby' (red, crimson and rose), raised at the Research Station, Boskoop, Holland and introduced to commerce in 1980, a hybrid between *Cytisus* × *praecox* and *Cytisus* 'Hollandia'; 'Burkwoodii' (cerise and maroon-red), raised by Burkwood and Skipwith; 'C.E. Pearson' (rose, yellow and red), raised by Watson's Nurseries, Killiney, Co. Dublin; 'Cornish Cream', (cream and yellow) which originated in Cornwall; 'Firefly' (yellow and rich mahogany-crimson), raised by the Daisy Hill Nursery of Newry, N. Ireland in around 1906; 'Golden Sunlight' (rich golden yellow), introduced by the Dutch nursery K. Wezelenburg & Sons of Hazerswoude in 1929; 'Hollandia' (a blend of salmon-pink and lilac-pink) which was raised at the Research Station, Boskoop, Holland and introduced to commerce in 1955, a hybrid of *C.* × praecox with *C.* 'Burkwoodii'; 'Killiney Red' (bright red), dwarf compact habit to 1m (3ft), raised by Watson's Nurseries of Killiney, Co. Dublin but the true plant is seldom seen; 'Lady Moore' (pinkish yellow and orange flame) also raised by Watson's Nurseries and named after Phylis, wife of Sir Frederick Moore (AM 1928); 'Lena' (ruby red and pale yellow), a compact and comparatively dwarf plant to 1.3m (4ft) which received a First Class Certificate from the RHS after trial at Wisley and was introduced to commerce around 1984; and 'Zeelandia' (pale lilac-pink and red), which was raised at the Research Station, Boskoop, Holland and introduced to commerce in 1955. It is of multiple parentage – (*C.* × praecox) × (*Cytisus* × *dallimorei*). Most of these are capable of reaching 2m (6ft) or so and bloom in late spring.

For smaller gardens the Warminster broom *C.* × praecox and its cultivars are among the most free-flowering of all garden shrubs. The typical plant has sulphur yellow flowers in late spring while those of 'Allgold' and 'Gold Spear' are rich yellow, and 'Albus' white. All these are spring flowering brooms flowering on the previous year's shoots. They are also fast growing and are liable to become leggy in time. If you can remember, it is worth pruning right from the word go by cutting back close to the base all, or at least some, of the flowering shoots immediately they are spent. On no account prune into the hard wood.

Propagation is by cuttings in late summer. Being resentful of disturbance, brooms are generally grown and supplied by nurserymen in pots and once planted, are best left alone.

Daphne collina

- HARDY
- SUN
- MOST WELL-DRAINED SOILS
- EVERGREEN
- ZONES 7–8

Daphne collina

Ever since *Daphne collina* was discovered in the hills above Naples in Italy in the eighteenth century its true status has been the subject of argument among experts. Even its introduction to British cultivation sometime in the middle of the eighteenth century is a source of debate. Most students of the genus are of the opinion that *D. collina* is no more than a local form of the more widespread *Daphne sericea*, differing in its usually more compact habit with wider and blunter leaves more densely hairy beneath and up to twice as many flowers in a cluster. This is certainly true of the plants in general cultivation which are clonal in nature, having been vegetatively propagated over many years.

Whatever its true botanical status and however much the experts may deliberate, gardeners are in no doubt as to its merits. It forms a densely branched dome-shaped bush of compact habit, averaging 45cm (18in) in height and up to twice as much across, densely clothed with neat glossy-topped, leathery, evergreen leaves up to 4cm (1in) long. The tubular flowers with a star-shaped mouth are a deep rose purple in colour, intensely fragrant and borne in terminal clusters in mid to late spring.

D. collina is tolerant of a wide range of soils – acid to alkaline – so long as they are reasonably fertile and well drained without drying out entirely in summer. It also demands a position in full sun and is ideal for the rock garden as well as a raised bed, large trough or stone container. In the wild, apparently, *D. collina* is found in rocky places on limestone formations with its head in the sun and its roots delving deeply into the cooler, moister soil below. I have seen *D. sericea* in similar situations in Crete.

It is hardy in all except the coldest areas of Britain where its foliage can be browned in severe winters. Like many others of its clan, it is subject to die-back usually as an old plant and affected branches should be cut cleanly away and burned. Sometimes die-back is progressive and the plant must then be removed completely and destroyed. Poor drainage, or alternatively lack of moisture in summer droughts, are a prime cause of distress. Other than this *D. collina* is a choice and reliable little evergreen, flowering even when quite young. Propagation is best done from cuttings in summer while grafting is often used by commercial growers. Seed, when available, is said to germinate easily.

Daphne collina
(**Family:** Thymelaeaceae)
Pronunciation: *dăf*-nay
Meaning: the Greek name for *Laurus nobilis*
Pronunciation: col-*ee*-na
Meaning: pertaining to hills.

Daphne pontica

Although it has been known in cultivation since the beginning of the nineteenth century, if not earlier, *Daphne pontica* is one of the most underrated shrubs in cultivation. Evergreen and hardy, with glossy leathery leaves and showers of elusively fragrant yellow green flowers in spring, it is an excellent choice for half-shade especially in woodland and will tolerate most soils though it prefers an acid

Daphne pontica
- HARDY
- SUN OR HALF-SHADE
- MOST SOILS
- EVERGREEN
- ZONES 7–8

one especially if there is humus and moisture available. It is a low, often spreading shrub to 1m (3ft) high eventually and up to twice as much across though generally much less. The curious rather spidery flowers in mid to late spring are not the most colourful in this genus yet they are not without charm. They are borne from the leaf axils at the base of the current year's growth and form loose crowded clusters, followed by black berries.

In the Hillier Arboretum in Hampshire a group of these shrubs was planted beneath a Japanese maple providing in spring a pleasant green and yellow undercover to the maple's purple canopy. Its tolerance of less than perfect conditions was amusingly referred to in a catalogue description by the late Sir Harold Hillier, 'will thrive under drip and in a heavy soil.' In the wild *D. pontica* is found in south-east Bulgaria and northern Turkey, from the vicinity of Istanbul along the Pontic Range into the Georgian Caucasus.

I first found *D. pontica* in the wild in May 1977 when accompanying a group of plant enthusiasts on a tour of northern Turkey and if it had not been for an encounter with some sheep guard-dogs I might not have seen it. We were climbing in the mountains around Lake Abant above Bolu in north-west Anatolia (Turkey in Asia) and with a colleague I was making my way across a grassy depression between two wooded hills where sheep were grazing. We hadn't gone 10 metres (30ft) when four large dogs (two from each flank) emerged from the trees and raced towards us. We briefly considered a quick retreat but the dogs would have considered us fair game and so we stayed put. For several minutes we remained stock still while the dogs – large brutes with rough, cream coloured hair and spiked collars – circled us baying all the while. We were wondering how best to extricate ourselves from this situation when there came a piercing whistle and we were relieved to see a shepherd approaching from out of a wood. Soon they were lying at his feet while he spoke to us in his native tongue, explaining, no doubt, that the dogs' bark was worse than their bite and that they would not hurt a fly! He pointed to a track leading into the wood indicating that we should take it and then with a smile and a wave of his hand he walked away, his dogs following on his heels but turning occasionally as if to make sure their master's instructions were being followed.

Still a little shaken by the experience, we followed the track for about half a mile before emerging from a grove of pine and on to a steep slope where *D. pontica* grew in some profusion. This seemed as good an excuse as any to sit down and eat the large oranges, chocolate and hazel-nuts we had been given for lunch that day while enjoying the daphne and its companions, mainly *Fritillaria pontica* and *Helleborus orientalis*. On several subsequent occasions we saw the daphne common in pine woodland or in scrub, its glossy evergreen leathery leaves forming dense ground-cover in places.

The flowers of some plants in the wild are pink tinted though the majority are yellowish green. *D. pontica* is not unlike our native spurge laurel *Daphne laureola* in some respects but is superior as a garden ornamental. It may be propagated by seed, cuttings in late summer, by layering or by grafting in late winter.

Daphne pontica
(**Family:** Thymelaeaceae)
Pronunciation: *dăf*-nay
Meaning: the Greek name for *Laurus nobilis*
Pronunciation: *pon*-ti-ka
Meaning: of Pontus (N.E. Turkey).

Dipelta floribunda

Dipelta floribunda
- HARDY
- SUN
- MOST SOILS
- ZONES 6–8

Generally regarded as one of the finest of all flowering deciduous shrubs, this splendid relative of the weigela is well worth considering for gardens of medium size and above where it can be given ample space to reach its maximum dimensions. This can be anything from 3–5m (10–20ft) depending on the situation. Once established it is a strong-growing shrub of upright habit, the older stems with pale brown bark which peels when old, providing an attractive winter feature. The leaves are of no special merit but the flowers more than make up for this when they crowd the branches in late spring borne on short branchlets along the one-year-old shoots. They are funnel-shaped and up to 3cm (1in) long, light pink in colour stained yellow in the throat. They are also fragrant and on a warm still afternoon or evening can be detected from some distance.

It is hardy enough but thrives best in the warmer regions where summer sun ripens growth. I first met with it in the University Botanic Garden, Cambridge but the finest specimen I ever saw, grew on the shallow chalk soil of Hilliers West Hill Nursery, Winchester where it had attained 6m (20ft) in the 1970s. This may well have been grown from E.H. Wilson's seed introduced from China's Hubei province in 1904. Two years previously he introduced living plants to the nursery of James Veitch and Sons at Coombe Wood in Surrey who offered it for sale for the first time in 1913.

Wilson found it on many occasions in north-west Hubei and in this same area some 80 years later I was fortunate in seeing it myself. It was quite common in the Wudang Shan (Wudang Mts) where it grew scattered in dense thickets together with a bewildering mixture of deutzias, roses, hypericums, shrubby honeysuckles and that lovely tree dogwood *Cornus kousa* var. *chinensis*. Sadly, despite its long sojourn in cultivation it is still rarely seen partly due no doubt to its difficulty in propagation, seeds are rarely produced here and cuttings taken in summer are slow to establish and not always successful.

Two other species *Dipelta ventricosa* and *Dipelta yunnanensis*, both Chinese, are occasionally seen in cultivation and are sometimes offered by specialist nurserymen, but though pretty when in flower they are no match for *D. floribunda*.

Dipelta floribunda
(**Family:** Caprifoliaceae)
Pronunciation: di-*pel*-ta
Meaning: from the Greek *di* (two) and *pelta* (a shield), referring to the conspicuous bracts which enclose the fruit
Pronunciation: flō-ri-*bun*-da
Meaning: flowering profusely.

Enkianthus perulatus

The enkianthus are a small group of deciduous shrubs from the Himalaya and east Asia, mainly represented in cultivation by *Enkianthus campanulatus*, a strong-growing shrub or small tree growing to 4m (13ft) high on average, with whorled branching forming in time tiers of growth. It is mainly grown for its numerous drooping clusters of small bell-shaped flowers in late spring. These can vary in colour from greenish white to red although they are commonly cream, heavily veined with red. As a bonus, the leaves (of some forms certainly) colour richly – yellow or red – before falling in autumn.

Similar in habit, though never so tall, is *Enkianthus cernuus* which is most often represented in British cultivation by the variety *rubens* with pendulous clusters of deep red bell-shaped flowers, fringed at the mouth. Different again is *Enkianthus perulatus* which is more suitable for smaller gardens being of dense twiggy, neater habit

Enkianthus perulatus

- HARDY
- HALF-SHADE
- MOIST BUT WELL-DRAINED LIME-FREE SOILS
- ZONES 6–8

and averaging 2m (6ft) in height, although much larger specimens have been recorded in old collections and in the wild. The flowers, unlike those of the previous two, are pitcher-shaped (narrowed at the mouth) and a clear white, appearing with the fresh green leaves in late spring. The latter are mainly clustered at the ends of the branches and usually provide a spectacular bonus in autumn when they turn a brilliant scarlet or purple-red.

All the above are native to Japan where they are found in hillside thickets as well as on the margins of woods and in clearings. *E. perulatus* was first introduced to British cultivation around 1869 and first offered by John Standish, nurseryman of Ascot, Berkshire, shortly after, while *E. campanulatus* was first introduced for Veitch's Coombe Wood nursery in Surrey by Charles Maries in 1880.

These three species are hardy and easy enough in cultivation so long as they are planted in a moist but well-drained acid soil, preferably one with plenty of humus. They are best given half-shade but will take full sun so long as the soil does not dry out in summer. They are charming shrubs of elegant habit and are suitable for woodland planting or with other members of *Ericaceae*, such as rhododendrons and azaleas, in borders and beds. Propagation is easy from seed (but seedlings variable in merit) or, less easily, by cuttings in summer.

Enkianthus perulatus
(**Family:** Ericaceae)
Pronunciation: eng-kee-*ănth*-us
Meaning: from the Greek *enkyos* (pregnant) and *anthos* (a flower), in *E. quinqueflorus*, the first species to be named, each flower appears to bear another inside it
Pronunciation: pe-ru-*lah*-tus
Meaning: with conspicuous bud scales.

Exochorda giraldii

Exochorda giraldii

- HARDY
- SUN OR HALF-SHADE
- MOIST BUT WELL-DRAINED PREFERABLY LIME-FREE SOIL
- ZONES 6–8

Apart from one comparatively slow-growing cultivar, the exochordas are not all that well known in gardens. There are but a handful of species most of them of large size 3–4m (10–13ft) at least, of which *Exochorda giraldii* lays claim to being the most desirable. When flowering it is breathtaking and for those with space to spare, it is a shrub well worth considering. Of vigorous but slender stemmed habit, it will easily reach 4m (13ft) or more. Its stems are more spreading than those of its equally desirable variety *wilsonii*, the thin-textured leaves of a fresh green with pink midrib and stalk. The pure white flowers are quite substantial 2.5–5cm (1-2in) across and are borne in racemes at the ends of the shoots in mid to late spring. They are particularly effective when seen against a dark background.

It is a native of Gansu province in China where it was first found by the Italian missionary Giuseppe Giraldi growing on rocks and cliffs, and was introduced to British cultivation via Germany in 1909, two years after the introduction of var. *wilsonii*. More suited to smaller gardens is *E.* 'The Bride' a lower growing selection of the hybrid *E.* × macrantha (*E. korolkowii* × E. racemosa) which was raised by the Dutch firm of F.J. Grootendorst in about 1938. Compared with others, this is a slow-growing exochorda, forming a dense mound 1.5–2m (5-6ft) eventually and as much or more across, with arching and semi-drooping branches sporting racemes of white flowers in mid to late spring. Compared with the larger growing exochordas, 'The Bride' lacks grace as a mature plant but it is reliable and free flowering and is impressive enough to have been recognised by the Royal Horticultural Society with an Award of Merit in 1973 and a First Class Certificate in 1983.

The exochordas enjoy best a sunny situation and a moist but well-drained fertile soil. They can be propagated from cuttings in summer whilst seed is the easiest method for the species.

Exochorda giraldii
(**Family:** Rosaceae)
Pronunciation: eks-ō-*kor*-da
Meaning: from the Greek *exo* (outside) and *chorda* (a cord), referring to fibres outside the placenta in the ovary
Pronunciation: ji-*räl*-dee-ee
Meaning: after Giuseppe Giraldi who introduced it.

Forsythia × intermedia 'Golden Nugget'

One of the most graphic ways of finding out which flowering shrubs have 'made it' in cultivation is to travel by rail. Peeking into other people's gardens from a passing train some would argue is one of the few redeeming features of rail travel today, for a gardener certainly. Depending on the route taken, the variety of gardens on offer is enormous, ranging from humble village plots to country estates and parks. And then there is suburbia! Travelling into London from Southampton, as I do fairly frequently, one comes to recognise the shrubs which dominate suburban gardens. Each season, each month even, provides its own specialities such as purple- and white-plumed lilacs in late spring and scarlet-berried firethorns in autumn. In this pageant of colour which lasts for much of the year, early to mid spring belongs to the ubiquitous but reliable forsythia whose golden blossoms erupting from naked pale brown branches bring welcome colour to countless gardens.

The vast majority of these forsythias belong to the hybrid *Forsythia × intermedia* which combines the Chinese species *Forsythia suspensa* and *Forsythia viridissima*. The last named is rarely seen in cultivation now except in its dwarf form 'Bronxensis', whilst *F. suspensa* (in its variety *sieboldii*) is still grown and recommended for large gardens where its rambling habit and long pendulous stems may be usefully employed to cover steep banks, arbours, outhouses and high walls. It is, however, a powerful shrub capable of reaching 9m (30ft) when trained to a support and must be regularly pruned if it is not to exceed its brief.

Both the above species were introduced into European cultivation in the first half of the last century and by 1900, several hybrids between these two had been recorded. The most important of these originated in the Botanical Garden at Gottingen, Germany in 1878 where self-sown seedlings were found by Herman Zabel, Director of the Municipal Garden in Munden. He published the name *F. × intermedia* in 1885 and several of these seedlings were later introduced to commerce by the Berlin firm of Späth. Seedlings and branch sports continued to appear and there is now a wide selection of named cultivars.

The most commonly grown cultivar in the North of England when I was a young man was 'Spectabilis', a vigorous shrub up to 3m (10ft) and as much across with flowers of a rich yellow, densely clustered along the branches. It was put into commerce by Späth at the beginning of this century and is still extensively planted, well deserving the Award of Merit and First Class Certificate given it by the Royal Horticultural Society in 1915 and 1935 respectively.

Even better to some eyes is 'Lynwood' which occurred as a branch sport on a bush of 'Spectabilis' growing in the garden at Lynwood, the home of a Miss Adair near Cookstown, Co. Tyrone. It was brought to the attention of the Slieve Donard nursery, Newcastle, Co. Down who propagated it and introduced it to commerce around 1948. Its flowers are the same colour as those of 'Spectabilis' but

Forsythia × intermedia
(**Family:** Oleaceae)
Pronunciation: for-*sieth*-ee-a
Meaning: after William Forsyth (1737–1804), Scottish gardener who became Superintendent of the Royal Garden at Kensington Palace
Pronunciation: in-ter-*med*-ee-a
Meaning: intermediate (between the parents).

larger. There are also several other relatively minor differences. It received an Award of Merit when shown before the RHS in 1956.

More recent in origin is 'Gold Nugget' which was raised in his garden by Reg Alford, one time foreman of Hilliers Eastleigh Nursery, Southampton. Over the years, Alf, as he is known to his friends, has raised numerous hybrids of hardy trees and shrubs and his experienced eyes have spotted many sports and seedlings which have since become established in cultivation. His forsythia was the result of crossing 'Arnold Giant' with an unnamed forsythia originally distributed to the trade, wrongly it appears, as 'Beatrix Farrand'. The cross was made in 1964 and from the resultant seedlings 'Gold Nugget' was selected and named. Slow to begin with but increasing in vigour to reach 2–2.6m (6–8ft) and as much across eventually, its leaves are sharply and boldly toothed, not unlike those of a nettle (*Urtica dioica*) in shape. The flowers meanwhile, nodding like golden snowdrops in bud, expand to 4–5cm (1½–2in) across, deep yellow with four, five or even six spreading lobes.

All the forsythias are hardy and easy in most soils and situations, acid or alkaline, sun or half-shade and may be propagated from cuttings in summer or by hardwood cuttings in late autumn or early winter. Most forsythias, being vigorous and often untidy in habit, respond well to pruning which consists of removing the oldest stems immediately after flowering.

Magnolia stellata 'Waterlily'

Of all the many lovely magnolias in cultivation *Magnolia stellata*, the star magnolia, is undoubtedly the one best suited for small gardens. It is a densely twiggy shrub and although some old specimens in cultivation have been known to achieve 6m (20ft) in height, by as much or more across, 2–3m (6–10ft) after 20 years is the average. The secret of its popularity with gardeners is twofold. First of all, it is amenable to most soils, although on chalky or sandy soils it benefits from a liberal mulching of organic material each year in spring. Second, it begins flowering from an early age and it is not uncommon to buy small contained specimens with up to a dozen buds.

The flowers, some 7.5cm (3in) across, are composed of numerous white or pink strap-shaped petals (tepals correctly) giving the characteristic bursting star effect, quite unlike the cup or goblet shape with which magnolias are commonly associated. They are also fragrant, the scent varying in intensity from plant to plant. The grey furry flower-buds are formed in late summer, opening the following spring when the branches are still leafless. In a warm spring they will begin opening earlier, although spring is their peak time. The leaves are around 10cm (4in) long and half as wide, turning yellow and bronze in autumn.

M. stellata is a native of Japan and was first introduced to Western cultivation by Dr George Hall of Rhode Island, New York in 1861.

Magnolia stellata
(**Family:** Magnoliaceae)
Pronunciation: măn-*yol*-ee-a, usually pronounced măg-*nol*-ee-a
Meaning: after Pierre Magnol (1638-1715), French professor of botany
Pronunciation: ste-*lah*-ta
Meaning: star-like (the flowers).

Above left: *Forsythia* × *intermedia* **'Gold Nugget'**
- HARDY
- SUN OR HALF-SHADE
- MOST SOILS
- ZONES 6–9

Above: *Magnolia stellata* **'Waterlily'**
- HARDY
- SUN OR HALF-SHADE
- MOST SOILS
- ZONES 5–9

Indeed, it was at one time named *Magnolia halliana* and was for a long time referred to, in the USA certainly, as Dr Hall's magnolia. Its first introduction to Britain, meanwhile, was probably that of the Veitch nursery collector Charles Maries in 1877. In the wild, it is found in a very restricted area in the mountains of southern Honshu where it occurs on the edges of streams and bogs, often accompanied by an alder, *Alnus hirsuta*, and *Ilex crenata*, a small leaved evergreen holly. Beyond its native locations it is a common Japanese garden plant having been cultivated there for centuries. Some students of magnolia regard it as no more than a variety of the more widespread *Magnolia kobus*, but having recently seen it for myself in the wild I am inclined to agree with those who maintain it is a distinct species.

Although the typical *M. stellata*, as seen in British cultivation, is quite satisfactory, there are available several named cultivars which have been selected for their improved ornamental effect. One of these is 'Waterlily', an outstanding magnolia for the small- to medium-sized garden, differing in its larger flowers with more numerous tepals. This plant with white flowers originated in the Boskoop nursery of Kluis and reached Britain via the Hillier Nurseries in 1952. To confuse matters, there are in addition three pink-flowered cultivars bearing this name all of which originated in the United States. None, however, is as yet generally available in the British trade.

'Centennial' is a fine white cultivar similar to our 'Waterlily' but more vigorous, raised at the Arnold Arboretum, Massachusetts, and named during their centennial year in 1972. Another American selection is 'Royal Star', a large flowered and vigorous cultivar which originated in John Vermeulan's old nursery on Long Island in 1947. Its large flowers have a faint blush on the outside at first, turning white later and opening about a week after those of the typical plant. Among the pink forms are 'Rosea', in which the flowers open blush pink and fade to white (the colour is more noticeable on old plants), 'Rosea King', similar in colour to 'Rosea' but flowers with a greater number of tepals (also freer-flowering) and 'Chrysanthemumiflora' which some magnolia connoisseurs consider the best pink *stellata* yet. It is only just becoming available in Britain.

Although hardy in cool temperate climates, *M. stellata* and its selections will sometimes suffer flower damage during severe late frosts but they are normally replaced by fast developing buds. Otherwise, it is an exemplary shrub of easy cultivation, more tolerant of wind than others of its clan. It can be propagated by seed when available while selected forms must be increased vegetatively either by cuttings in summer or by grafting. Although it makes an excellent front of the border shrub in early life its ultimate size demands a situation with plenty of 'elbow room'. It makes an even better specimen shrub in the middle of the lawn and flowers best in full sun or half-shade.

Osmanthus delavayi

Jean Marie Delavay was one of the most famous of the French missionary naturalists working in China during the last century. Born in Abondance in the Haute-Savoie, he was posted to China in 1867 at the age of 33 and for the first few years served in a small town in Guangdong province near the capital Guangzhou (Canton). He was then transferred to a small town in the hills north of Dali in Yunnan province where he remained for almost ten years. In 1888 he contracted bubonic plague and although he survived he suffered from the effects of it for the rest of his life.

Unlike his contemporary the Abbé David, who was a naturalist with wide interests, Delavay specialised in botany and during his years in Yunnan he travelled extensively, collecting and drying the plants he discovered. He despatched a total of 200,000 specimens to the Paris Museum, an incredible number which included many plants new to science. It has been claimed that more worthwhile garden plants were first discovered by Delavay than by any other botanist. Sadly, although he also sent home many seeds, a great number were lost through mismanagement and neglect.

One of these seed lots belonged to an evergreen shrub with sweetly scented flowers which he had discovered in woodland in the mountains above Dali. The seeds had been despatched in 1890 to the French nurseryman Maurice de Vilmorin who further distributed them. Incredibly, only one seedling resulted and as this developed, its shoots were grafted onto stocks of privet and *Phillyrea latifolia*, a related evergreen. Thus, plant by plant, it became safely established

Osmanthus delavayi
(**Family:** Oleaceae)
Pronunciation: os-*mănth*-us
Meaning: from Greek *osme* (fragrance) and *anthos* (a flower), the fragrant flowers
Pronunciation: del-a-*vay*-ee
Meaning: after the Abbé Delavay (1834–1895) who first introduced this shrub to France in 1890.

Osmanthus delavayi
- HARDY
- SUN OR HALF-SHADE
- MOST SOILS
- EVERGREEN
- ZONES 8-10

in cultivation until by 1911 it was being featured in French nursery catalogues and three years later it was given an Award of Merit by the Royal Horticultural Society. By this time, Père Delavay's shrub had been given a name *Osmanthus delavayi* one of many plants to bear his name. Today, *O. delavayi* is fairly widespread in Western cultivation, principally as a result of further seed introductions by the Scottish plant hunter George Forrest in the first quarter of the present century.

In cultivation it makes a large shrub up to 3m (10ft) and as much through, twice this in the sheltered woodland gardens of Cornwall and similarly mild locations elsewhere. The arching downy branches bear pairs of small rounded neatly toothed leaves which are leathery and a dark glossy green above while the white flowers, although small individually, are produced in great numbers in the leaf axils creating charming sprays and wreaths, richly scented in the middle of spring.

It is hardy enough in cool temperate climates but is subject to damage, usually leaf scorch, in cold inland areas during severe winters. It is suited to most soils acid or alkaline preferring, however, one well supplied with humus and sufficiently moist in summer to prevent drying out. A position in sun or half-shade is appreciated. Propagation is by cuttings in late summer.

Photinia × fraseri 'Red Robin'

Photinia × fraseri
'Red Robin'
- HARDY
- SUN OR HALF-SHADE
- MOST SOILS
- EVERGREEN
- ZONES 8–10

If you are an admirer of *Pieris* 'Forest Flame' but cannot enjoy it in your own garden because of an alkaline soil then you might consider one of the evergreen hybrid photinias of which several are now available in cultivation. The three main species involved are *Photinia davidiana, Photinia glabra* and *Photinia serratifolia* (formerly *serrulata*). The first of these is better known as *Stranvaesia davidiana* but it is so closely allied botanically to photinia that most authorities now regard them as inseparable. A native of China, where it is widely distributed in the south and west, *P. davidiana* was first found by the French missionary Armand David after whom it is named. It was not established in cultivation, however, until the introductions of E.H. Wilson in the first decade of the present century. Since then it has become a widely grown shrub or small tree admired as much for its red berries as for its evergreen foliage.

Less common in gardens is *P. serratifolia* a more robust shrub or small tree capable of 9m (30ft) or more in a warm sheltered position especially against a wall or in the woodland gardens of the south-west and west. Like *P. davidiana*, a native of China, *P. serratifolia* was first introduced as long ago as 1804 by a Captain Kirkpatrick of the East India Company yet it remains relatively uncommon in gardens. Its tolerance of frost is quite remarkable, the early emerging growths surviving all but the severest weather conditions and even when badly damaged it usually breaks again from the old wood.

Not so amenable to cold is *P. glabra*, a native of Japan and China, which in its cultivar 'Rubens' is commonly planted as a hedge in Mediterranean areas. In Britain it is mostly seen in the south and west and elsewhere in warm pockets where it forms a dense leafy bush up to 3m (10ft) high eventually and as much across. It is easily maintained at a smaller size, however, by an annual light pruning in summer after the spring growth has slowed and firmed.

Better known in today's gardens than either of the last two species is the hybrid between them known as *Photinia × fraseri*. This is named after the Fraser Nurseries of Birmingham, Alabama where it first occurred as a chance seedling in around 1940. It was introduced to commerce in 1952 and has since been vegetatively propagated to such an extent that it is now a 'bread and butter' plant of many nurseries in southern USA. It is a strong growing shrub to 5m (16ft) or more in height and as much across with firm, dark green, leathery leaves which flush bronze-red in spring hence the common name Red-tip in the United States. To distinguish this cultivar from others of the same parentage it was given the name 'Birmingham'.

Although 'Birmingham' is available in Britain the hybrid is more commonly represented here by 'Robusta' introduced by the Hazlewood Nursery of Sydney, Australia while 'Red Robin' is of New Zealand origin. The former is more inclined towards *P. serratifolia* in leaf while the young foliage is coppery red. 'Red Robin', meanwhile, has the brightest young foliage of them all, more red than copper and very striking in spring. All the cultivars of *P. × fraseri* are similar in vigour and habit, fairly open and erect as young plants gradually filling out and becoming quite dense and relatively compact as they mature. Providing they have had a warm summer the previous year to ripen growth, they produce an abundance of flattened heads of small white flowers in late spring – earlier or later depending on the seasonal variations.

All the above photinias are suitable for a wide range of soils excepting those ill drained. They are particularly useful for alkaline soils and while their young growths are less brilliant than those of *Pieris* 'Forest Flame', they are at least more frost hardy and their effect more lasting. They are ideal specimen evergreens for lawns and make good screening plants for all year round effect. Being gross feeders they naturally appreciate rich soil or an annual mulch of organic material. One serious problem likely to affect them is fireblight but so far this has been more troublesome with *P. davidiana* than any of the others. They can be propagated by cuttings in late summer while the species are easily grown from seed when available.

Photinia × fraseri
(**Family:** Rosaceae)
Pronunciation: fō-*tin*-ee-a
Meaning: from the Greek *photos* (light) referring to the shining leaves of some species
Pronunciation: *fray*-za-ree
Meaning: after Fraser's Nursery, Alabama where this hybrid was first raised.

Pieris 'Forest Flame'

The Chinese town of Yangbi in western Yunnan is a relatively small hard-working community whose main claim to fame rests on its importance as the walnut capital of China. Walnut trees (*Juglans regia*) are planted in their thousands, some of great age, in the hills around and their nuts are gathered and exported to other provinces and abroad – to Europe for instance. It lies in a valley not far from the Burma Road and is frowned upon by the long bulk of the Cangshan, a range of mountains better known in plant hunting circles as the Tali Range. From these mountains earlier this century famous plant hunters including Joseph Rock and George Forrest introduced some of the finest ornamentals to our gardens.

Forrest is particularly associated with the Cangshan for it was here in 1906 that he first found the evergreen which now bears his name *Pieris formosa* var. *forrestii*. The species itself is widely distributed in the wild in the eastern Himalaya and south-west China, where it is found as a large shrub up to 9m (30ft) high, or as a small tree, in sheltered woodland. Its young growths may vary from bronze to a coppery red emerging at the same time as or after the drooping bunches of small white pitcher-shaped flowers. Forrest's variety, however, is superior in the brilliant crimson shade of its young growths and is more often planted as a consequence.

Seed sent back by Forrest produced seedlings varying slightly in character and several of these have been named. One such is 'Wakehurst' which was awarded a First Class Certificate by the Royal Horticultural Society in 1930 when shown from Wakehurst Place in Sussex. This is the most popular of the selections for medium-sized to large gardens reaching 5–6m (16–20ft), and almost as much across when sheltered. Its brilliant young growths and white flowers like lily of the valley normally appear together, usually from late spring into early summer and a large plant at its peak is very impressive. Flowering, by the way, is variable; profuse some years less so in others. The crimson young growths meanwhile fade to crimson pink then through pale yellow to a chlorotic green and finally green.

'Jermyns' is another selection of var. *forrestii*, distinct in the winter effect of its drooping panicles. The flowering branches and buds which, as in all pieris, are formed the previous summer, are coloured a rich reddish brown, the flowers later opening white with dark red calyces – a charming contrast. It was raised as a seedling in the Jermyns nursery of Messrs Hillier near Romsey, Hampshire in 1950 and received an Award of Merit from the RHS in 1959.

The only drawback to growing 'Wakehurst' and 'Jermyns' is the tendency for their young growths to be damaged by late frosts. If they escape unharmed then 'Wakehurst' especially is magnificent but it is a risk one has to take. More satisfactory for general cultivation, therefore, especially if a nice sheltered or woodland site is unavailable, are 'Firecrest' and 'Forest Flame' which are hybrids of *P. formosa* var. *forrestii* with the hardier *Pieris japonica*

Pieris
(**Family:** Ericaceae)
Pronunciation: *pee*-e-ris
Meaning: from *Pierides*, a name of the Muses (goddesses of the arts).

from Japan. The first of these was named by Messrs John Waterer and Sons and Crisp of Bagshot, Surrey, who had grown it since the 1930s at least as *P. formosa* under Forrest collection No. 8945. It is a splendid evergreen of upright growth with drooping tassels of white flowers in late winter and early spring followed in mid to late spring by young growths that are red, pink, peach and yellow shades depending on stage of development. These are surprisingly frost tolerant often at their best when those of the larger leaved *P. formosa* var. *forrestii* and its selections have been blackened. It will reach 5m (16ft) at least eventually and half this across.

As valuable in garden terms is 'Forest Flame'. A self-sown seedling found in the Sunningdale Nurseries, Surrey in 1952, it differs mainly from 'Firecrest' in its neater, less vigorous more compact habit. The young growths are crimson then deep rose-red in mid to late spring paling to salmon pink through creamy-yellow to green. The flowers appearing in early spring are white but less freely borne than those of 'Firecrest'. Not surprisingly, both these cultivars were given an Award of Merit for their young foliage when shown before the Royal Horticultural Society in 1973. 'Firecrest' also earned an Award of Merit for its flowers in 1981.

In recent years, 'Forest Flame' has produced variegated sports on several occasions in different gardens. One of these introduced by the Dutch nursery firm of A.J. Kuijf and Son of Boskoop in 1985 has much smaller narrower leaves than the type and they are marbled green and grey with an irregular white margin. It has been named *Pieris* 'Flaming Silver', a reference to the brightly coloured young

Pieris 'Forest Flame'

- HARDY, BUT SUBJECT TO DAMAGE FROM SPRING FROSTS
- SUN OR HALF-SHADE
- LIME-FREE SOILS
- EVERGREEN
- ZONES 7–8

growths against the variegation of the mature foliage. It is more vigorous than the better known *P. japonica* 'Variegata' and shows every intention of making a compact medium-sized to large shrub. A similar sport originating in the garden of John Waterer at Tilford in Surrey has been named 'Robinswood'.

Just as desirable is *P. japonica* which, in one form or another, is the most commonly cultivated pieris in Britain. The type, a native of Japan and eastern China, is a large evergreen shrub to 3m (10ft) of compact mounded habit with dark glossy evergreen leaves and terminal clusters of drooping racemes 7.5–15cm (3–6in) long. The individual flowers are small, white and pitcher shaped and are at their best from the end of winter into early or mid spring. They are also sweetly scented. There are now numerous cultivars. These include 'Blush' with rose-pink flowers on a bush up to 1.7m (5ft) high and wide. It was introduced to commerce by Messrs Hillier in the 1960s. 'Pink Delight' is similar but to all accounts better. 'Flamingo' was raised in the USA and introduced to commerce in 1961. It is a tall shrub to 3m (10ft) with flowers of a rich pink shading to white at the base which are borne in long drooping racemes. It received an Award of Merit from the RHS in 1981. Similar, but with flowers of an even darker red is 'Valley Valentine'. It was raised by R. Ticknor of the Horticultural Research Station, Aurora, Oregon, and was introduced to commerce in 1978. 'White Cascade' is another American selection, a strong growing shrub with unusually long trusses of pure white flowers. 'Purity', one of the best of its kind, is a compact shrub to 1.3m (4ft) or so high. It flowers from an early age, the pure white flowers in erect racemes appearing late in the season (early to mid spring). It received an Award of Merit from the RHS in 1977 and was introduced to commerce by the Crown Estate Commissioners, Windsor Great Park. 'Grayswood' is a dome-shaped bush to 1.7m (5ft) high, eventually, with long drooping racemes of white flowers freely borne. It was raised at Grayswood Hill, the late Geoffrey Pilkington's garden in Haslemere, Surrey. 'White Pearl' is a very fine pieris of dwarf habit, to 1m (3ft), with dense erect panicles of white flowers, ideal for the really small garden. It was raised in the nursery of a Mr Kubas of Snohomish near Seattle, USA, and first introduced to commerce by Messrs Verboom of Boskoop, Holland, in 1982. Even better is 'Debutante', raised at the Research Station in Boskoop from seed collected by Robert and Jelena de Belder of Kalmthout, Belgium, in 1970 on the mountains of Yakushima, an island in southern Japan. It differs from 'White Pearl' in its denser more compact habit, neater foliage and later flowering. Two lovely silvery cream variegated cultivars are 'Variegata', slow growing and compact up to 4m (13ft) eventually, and 'Little Heath', even slower growing to 1m (3ft) eventually.

All the above enjoy a moist but well-drained acid or at least lime-free soil in sun or half-shade and appreciate an annual mulching with leaf mould or similar. They will tolerate pruning should this be necessary, as for instance after periods of severe winter weather when even the hardier among them may suffer damage. Propagation is by cuttings in late summer and autumn.

Prunus tenella

Known as the Dwarf Russian almond, *Prunus tenella* is one of the most floriferous and reliable of the shrubby members of this genus. A native of south-west Russia and parts of central and south-east Europe, it is generally low growing to 1m (3ft), occasionally taller, of bushy suckering habit with numerous erect, slender stems. These are wreathed in mid spring, before the glossy green leaves appear, with deep pink to rose-red flowers 1.5cm (1/2in) or more across. Most forms I have seen in cultivation have been attractive while those selections with richer coloured flowers are exceptional. Such an example is 'Fire Hill' which was introduced from the Balkans by Lady Alice Martineau (1866–1956). It received an Award of Merit from the Royal Horticultural Society in 1959. There is also a form 'Alba' with white flowers.

Cultivated in England, certainly since the late seventeenth century, *P. tenella* is a tough, hardy little shrub suitable for the front of a border or bed in full sun. It appears to be amenable to most soils, acid or alkaline, but a watch must be kept on its wandering tendencies when planted among other small shrubs or low perennials. It grows particularly well in the drier south-east of Britain and I remember it attracting plenty of admirers in the University Botanic Garden, Cambridge when I was a student there in the early 1960s. It can be propagated by cuttings in summer or by layering. Rooted suckers can also be easily detached.

Another member of the genus equally suited to small gardens is *Prunus glandulosa*, a native of north-east China, Korea and south-east Siberia, long cultivated in Japan. Although the wild plant with single pink flowers is sometimes grown, the species is mainly represented in gardens by two double-flowered cultivars 'Alba Plena' and 'Rosea

Prunus tenella
(**Family:** Rosaceae)
Pronunciation: *proo*-nus
Meaning: Latin name for the plum tree
Pronunciation: te-*nel*-la
Meaning: dainty.

Prunus tenella
- HARDY
- SUN
- MOST SOILS
- ZONES 3–7

Plena'. Both are normally seen as neat bushy shrubs 1–1.5m (3–5ft) high, the slender stems clothed with finely toothed, willow-like leaves. The flowers are borne in late spring on the previous year's wood, wreathing the stems in exquisite fashion. Those of 'Alba Plena' are 2.5–3cm (1–1¼in) across, multi-petalled and white, while 'Rosea Plena' has similar flowers but pink in colour. The latter is sometimes grown under the name 'Sinensis'.

Both had been cultivated in China and Japan for a very long time before they were introduced to cultivation in the West. 'Rosea Plena' is said to have arrived here in the second half of the eighteenth century, in 1774 perhaps, while 'Alba Plena' was probably first introduced in 1846 by Robert Fortune who purchased it from a Shanghai Nursery. In the Victorian and Edwardian eras these double-flowered prunus were commonly potted and forced into early flower under glass for use in the home and conservatory and this technique is still practised, though to a much lesser extent, today.

There is no question that they flower best after a good summer has ripened the wood and initiated flower buds, and outside they are often planted and trained against a sunny wall to help achieve this. They are perfectly all right, however, as free standing shrubs in a sunny border or bed being unfussed as to soil – acid or alkaline – so long as it is well drained and provided with humus. In order to encourage more prolific flowering, and at the same time, a more shapely habit, the flowering shoots should be removed to within two or three buds of their base immediately the flowers have faded. Pruning clear away from the base is sometimes necessary to deal with shoots which have been killed by a wilt disease, otherwise they present no serious problems in their cultivation and can be propagated by cuttings in summer or by layering.

Both these shrubs have received the Award of Merit from the RHS; 'Alba Plena' in 1950 and 'Rosea Plena' in 1968. They are two of the finest flowering shrubs for the small garden.

Rhododendron 'P.J. Mezitt'

Apart from the ubiquitous 'ponticum', the rhododendron I most clearly remember from childhood is *Rhododendron*. 'Praecox' which was once everybody's favourite in the North of England. It was planted in gardens large and small and the few nurseries in the area seemed to grow nothing else. Its popularity rested on three things; namely its hardiness, its relatively compact habit and its reliable flowering when there was little else in the garden. It was introduced to commerce in 1860 by Isaac Davies of Larkfield Nursery, Wavetree, near Liverpool, which no doubt explains why it was so common in Lancashire and Cheshire gardens.

According to Bean, Davies made the hybrid in 1853 by placing the pollen of the then recently introduced *Rhododendron ciliatum* from the Himalayas onto *Rhododendron dauricum* which had been grown

Rhododendron 'PJ Mezitt'

- HARDY
- SUN OR HALF-SHADE
- LIME-FREE SOILS
- EVERGREEN
- ZONES 5–8

in English gardens since 1780. Seedlings from the cross were already flowering by 1858 and its future as a garden shrub was assured. It is a densely twigged bush of upright habit with small dark glossy green leaves, aromatic when crushed, which persist through all but the severest winters and are usually present when the flowers open in late winter or early spring. These are funnel shaped almost 5cm (2in) across and a striking rose-purple. Although borne in twos and threes from buds towards the ends of the shoots, they are produced in such numbers that a bush in full bloom creates a rich and cheerful splash even from a distance.

Like many other early flowering rhododendrons, however, 'Praecox' sometimes suffers from frost damage and it pays, therefore, to give it, where possible, a position sheltered from persistent cold winds and to avoid likely frost pockets. Some of the best flowering specimens I have seen enjoyed some light shade but not so much that flowering potential is affected. It is sometimes planted as a hedge and poorly shaped specimens can be pruned if necessary to encourage bushier growth. Well-budded sprigs can be brought indoors in the New Year where they readily flower. It was awarded a First Class Certificate by the Royal Horticultural Society in 1978 and, in common with most rhododendrons, requires a lime-free soil.

In areas where early frosts are a real problem the American hybrid 'P.J. Mezitt' is recommended. Described by the Coxes in their Encyclopaedia, as one of the hardiest hybrids ever raised, it is the result of a cross between *R. minus* 'Carolinianum' and *R. dauricum* raised by P.J. Mezitt of the Weston Nurseries, Maine, USA and introduced to commerce in 1959. The evergreen leaves are rounded and aromatic, turning a mahogany colour in winter while the long lasting flowers are rose-purple in late winter and early spring. It is claimed to be scorch, wind and drought resistant and is recommended for a sunny site where it will develop into an upright compact rounded bush of excellent habit. It was given an Award of Merit by the RHS in 1972.

Rhododendron
(**Family:** Ericaceae)
Pronunciation: ro-do-*den*-dron
Meaning: the Greek name for *Nerium oleander* from *rhodo* (red) and *dendron* (a tree)

Rhododendron wardii

If ever a plant hunter deserved to be knighted it must surely have been Frank Kingdon-Ward who died in 1958 at the age of 73. An explorer, geographer and prolific author, he had the distinction of being the longest serving professional plant collector in history. Working for a succession of sponsors and subscribers beginning with E.K. Bulley in 1909, he mounted no fewer than 24 expeditions to Asia most of them in Tibet, Burma, Assam and Yunnan and he was planning yet another at the time of his death. He made a great number of seed and plant collections especially primulas and lilies but the plant for which he is best remembered is the blue poppy *Meconopsis betonicifolia* which he was the first to introduce into cultivation. He was also fond of rhododendrons and was responsible for

introducing seed of numerous species, sometimes in superior forms to those already in cultivation from previous collectors. Several of his rhododendrons were new to cultivation of which one *Rhododendron wardii* has been described as incomparable.

It is an evergreen shrub up to 5m (16ft) although there are smaller forms in cultivation more suitable where space is restricted. Its leaves vary from rounded to egg-shaped, always neat and of a rich green while the bell-shaped flowers are pure yellow, sometimes with a crimson stain in the throat. They are carried in loose trusses in late spring and when a plant is in full bloom it is a joy to see. Seed was first collected by Kingdon-Ward in 1913 on the Doker La, a mountain range in north-west Yunnan, China and in the same year it was collected by George Forrest only 120 miles to the east. Its distribution is wide, from south-west Sichuan westward through north-west Yunnan into south-east Tibet where it was collected much later by Ludlow and Sherriff. In the wild it grows in hillside thickets and occasionally in coniferous or deciduous woodland.

Rhododendron wardii

- TENDER WHEN YOUNG
- HALF-SHADE
- LIME-FREE SOILS
- EVERGREEN
- ZONES 7–8

Apart from commemorating a remarkable man, *R. wardii* is one of the finest of its kind for woodland gardens or elsewhere given light shade and protection from cold winds. It is regarded by no less an authority than Peter Cox as the best yellow-flowered species for general cultivation though the flowers are variable in depth of colour and frost hardiness – those collected by Frank Ludlow and George Sherriff being most satisfactory on this account. It can be propagated by seed or selected forms by cuttings in late summer.

R. wardii is a parent of many fine hybrids, including 'Crest' and 'Hotei'. The former (*wardii* × 'Lady Bessborough') was raised by Lionel de Rothschild at Exbury Gardens near Southampton and was introduced to commerce in 1953, in which year it received a First Class Certificate from the RHS. It is a tall shrub of upright habit and is most suitable for sheltered, especially woodland, gardens as it is a little tender when young. The leaves are deep shining green while the long lasting, clear primrose-yellow flowers, orange in bud, are carried in an elegant truss in late spring. 'Hotei' ('Goldsworth Orange' × (*soulei* × *wardii*)) is an American-raised hybrid introduced to commerce in 1968. It is named after a Japanese god and has flowers of a rich yellow with deeper shading borne in bold trusses in late spring. It does best in half-shade and needs good drainage. The habit is dense.

At the other end of the scale is another Kingdon-Ward introduction, *Rhododendron pemakoense* which is one of the most free flowering of all dwarf species. It can reach 60cm (2ft) by more across, eventually forming a low mound of dense sometimes suckering habit clothed with small evergreen leaves, brown scaly beneath. The flowers, large for the size of plant, are broadly funnel shaped up to 5cm (2in) across and of a pale pinkish purple or similar. They are carried alone or in pairs at the tips of the shoots in early and mid spring often so freely that they hide the leaves.

Their earliness can be their undoing for they are liable to damage by frost should the weather turn nasty. No frost, and this is one of the most desirable and colourful dwarf rhododendrons in cultivation especially suited to the peat garden or rock garden (lime-free soil of course). *R. pemakoense* was found by Kingdon-Ward in 1924 growing on steep, damp moss-clad rocks and rills in the Tsangpo Gorge in the Tibetan province of Pemako and received an Award of Merit from the Royal Horticultural Society in 1928. It can be propagated from seed or by cuttings in late summer.

Rhododendron wardii
(**Family:** Ericaceae)
Pronunciation: ro-do-*den*-dron
Meaning: the Greek name for *Nerium oleander* from *rhodo* (red) and *dendron* (a tree)
Pronunciation: *wor*-dee-ee
Meaning: after Frank Kingdon-Ward who discovered this species.

Rhododendron williamsianum

Wa Shan (now called by the Chinese Ying Jin) is a mountain in western Sichuan which was first made known to the West through the plant introductions of E.H. Wilson, although he was not the first European to ascend it. He first climbed it in 1903 on his expedition for the Veitch Nurseries in Surrey and again in 1908 for the Arnold

Arboretum in Massachusetts. On both occasions he was impressed by the mountain's bulk and shape. It is not that Wa Shan is high by Chinese standards – somewhere in excess of 3,000m (10,000ft) – rather that it dominates the surrounding countryside, from whence it is perceived as a flat-topped massif with almost sheer sides. It consists of two tiers, the upper storey being a series of 12 to 14 limestone precipices rising one above another and the only routes to the summit in Wilson's day certainly were by narrow tracks.

The thing that most struck Wilson about Wa Shan's flora was the preponderance of rhododendrons growing there. He estimated that 99 per cent of the summit vegetation consisted of members of this genus. He made many new discoveries there, including on his second visit in June 1908 a charming rhododendron which he later named *Rhododendron williamsianum* after one of his earlier sponsors J.C. Williams of Caerhays Castle in Cornwall. It occurred in the thickets covering the cliffs in the upper part of the mountain and was in flower. The following October he returned for its seed. Since Wilson's discovery this species has also been found on Wa Shan's sister mountain, the celebrated Emei Shan (Mt Omei). On neither, however, is it common.

Rhododendron williamsianum

- HARDY, BUT NEEDS SHELTER FROM COLD WINDS
- SUN OR HALF-SHADE
- LIME-FREE SOILS
- EVERGREEN
- ZONES 6–8

In cultivation *R. williamsianum* is valued for its dense compact often dome-shaped habit, which can be anything from 60cm–1.7m (2–5ft) eventually, and as much or more across. Just as characteristic and attractive are its small neat rounded leaves which vary from bronze to chocolate brown when young. Indeed, it is worth growing as a foliage subject alone. The pale pink to rose bell-shaped flowers from darker buds add considerably to its appearance when they appear in few-flowered trusses from the tips of the branches in mid to late spring. If it has one weakness it is the susceptibility of its flowers and young growths to spring frosts, but the risk is worth taking in all but the coldest areas. Some clones are later into growth than others and these are the ones to go for if hardiness is a consideration. It received an Award of Merit from the Royal Horticultural Society in 1938.

R. williamsianum as a parent has resulted in several lovely and garden worthy hybrids over the years including: 'Humming Bird' (with *Rhododendron haematodes*), with flowers of cherry red (in the best forms) in mid spring; 'Temple Belle' (with *Rhododendron orbiculare*) with persian rose to pale pink flowers (depending on form) in mid to late spring; 'Bow Bells' (with *Rhododendron 'Corona'*), flowers light pink, darker on reverse from deep pink buds, young growths reddish bronze also mid to late spring, Award of Merit 1935; 'Cowslip' (with *R. wardii*), flowers pale primrose yellow to cream with pink or red markings in late spring which received an Award of Merit 1937; and 'Brocade', a fairly vigorous hybrid of its kind, with frilly peach pink flowers and a rich green foliage. All five are fairly easy to root from cuttings in late summer (as is *R. williamsianum*) and compact and dome shaped in habit. They prefer shelter from cold winds and sun or light shade. Plants grown in too much shade tend to lose their shape and are often less free flowering.

Rhododendron williamsianum
(**Family:** Ericaceae)
Pronunciation: ro-do-*den*-dron
Meaning: the Greek name for *Nerium oleander* from *rhodo* (red) and *dendron* (a tree)
Pronunciation: wil-yămz-ee-*ah*-num
Meaning: after J.C. Williams of Caerhays Castle, Cornwall.

Rhododendron yakushimanum

No other rhododendron in recent years has caused as much excitement and feverish activity in the breeding world as *Rhododendron yakushimanum*. Its combination of neat compact habit, small size, excellent foliage and rounded trusses of pristine white flowers from pink buds is as near to perfect as is possible in a rhododendron. Add to this its hardiness and amenable nature and you can understand why it has been a godsend to rhododendron breeders who seem to have crossed it with everything under the sun to produce a myriad hybrids some of which, mercifully, have inherited yakushimanum's quality while others most certainly have not.

Despite the undoubted merits of the best yakushimanum hybrids, and 'Hydon Dawn' is one, I would plump for the original species every time, especially if your garden is none-too-large. I

Rhododendron yakushimanum
(**Family:** Ericaceae)
Pronunciation: ro-do-*den*-dron
Meaning: the Greek name for *Nerium oleander* from *rhodo* (red) and *dendron* (a tree)
Pronunciation: ya-koo-shee-*mah*-num
Meaning: of Yakushima, an island off south Japan.

have a specimen in an island bed in my front lawn which it shares with a winter-flowering heath *Erica carnea* 'Myretoun Ruby'. This particular plant, now a respectable dome of 60 x 90cm (2 x 3ft), is descended by cuttings from one of two plants introduced to Exbury Gardens in Hampshire in either 1934 or 1936 (accounts vary on this). These plants were sent by a well-known Japanese nurseryman the late Koichiro Wada of Hakoneya Nurseries, Numazushi. One of these plants was subsequently sent to the Royal Horticultural Society's garden at Wisley where it remains to this day. As an illustration of its rate of growth, in 1947 the Wisley plant measured 75 x 105 cm ($2^1/2$ x $3^1/2$ft), 28 years later it had increased to 1.6m x 2.3m (4ft 8in x 7ft). In 1947 it was exhibited at the Chelsea Flower Show and was awarded a First Class Certificate. This plant, from which mine originated, was subsequently named 'Koichiro Wada' in honour of its sender and

Rhododendron Yakushimanum

- HARDY
- SUN OR HALF-SHADE
- LIME-FREE SOILS
- EVERGREEN
- ZONES 5–8

is now stocked by a number of nurserymen, sometimes under the entry *R. yakushimanum* FCC Form.

In the wild this lovely species is restricted to Yakushima, a small mountainous island some 70km (43 miles) south of Kyushu, the southernmost of the four main islands of Japan. There, according to Peter Barnes, the Royal Horticultural Society's botanist at Wisley, it grows in alpine meadows above the forest in company with *Juniperus chinensis* var. *sargentii*, *Pseudosasa owatarii* (a dwarf bamboo) and other shrubs, together forming a fascinating patchwork quilt no higher than one's knee. It is a difficult rocky terrain at times obscured by mist, at others swept by strong winds and with an annual rainfall of 7,000mm (276in). Not surprisingly it grows well in British conditions so long as the soil is lime free. Other than that, it is happy in full sun or half-shade and makes an excellent 'spotplant' in the heather garden or among dwarf or creeping, especially ericaceous, plants or conifers. This shrub also does well in a container so long as it is not cramped, a fact which has not been lost on those gardening on chalk or limestone soils.

The hard, leathery evergreen leaves up to 9cm (3$^{1}/_{2}$in) long are glossy green above, the margins curved under to protect the thick pelt of light buff to fawn wool below. The bell-shaped flowers in dense rounded heads open from rose coloured buds to pale pink or white (pure white in 'Koichiro Wada' and 'Exbury Form') during late spring. Even young plants produce flowers. Propagation is by seed or, with difficulty, by cuttings in late summer. 'Koichiro Wada' is still largely grafted by nurserymen on to the common *Rhododendron ponticum* to which, of course, it is closely related botanically. Interestingly, the hybrids of *R. yakushimanum* root more readily than the type. Among the best are 'Vintage Rose' (*yakushimanum* × ('Jalisco Eclipse' × 'Fusileer')) with flowers in a large domed head of a rose-pink, deeper at the centre, which fade to near white. It also has excellent foliage. It was raised by Waterer Sons and Crisp of Bagshot, Surrey and was introduced to the trade in 1979. 'Surrey Heath' ((*facetum* × *'Fabia'*) × (*yakushimanum* × 'Britannia')) also has flowers of a rose-pink which are slightly spotted orange over a creamy yellow centre, fading to a two-tone effect. This was another Waterer introduction in 1975. 'Percy Wiseman' has flowers of a peach-pink fading to creamy white with a yellow throat and green marks, with good foliage. It was raised by and named after Messrs Waterer's late propagator and introduced to commerce in 1971. 'Caroline Allbrook' (*yakushimanum* × 'Purple Splendour') has flowers of a lavender-rose at first with a paler centre which fade to a very pale lavender, frilled at the margins. It is very free flowering and was raised by Hydon Nurseries of Godalming, Surrey and introduced to commerce in 1975. It received an Award of Merit from the RHS in 1977. From the same 'stable' is 'Hydon Dawn' (*yakushimanum* × 'Springbok') which was introduced to commerce in 1969 and received a First Class Certificate after Trial at Wisley in 1987. It has frilled flowers of pale pink fading to white. It is an excellent hybrid; one of the best of its kind.

Skimmia × confusa
'Kew Green'

- HARDY
- SUN OR HALF-SHADE
- MOST SOILS
- EVERGREEN
- ZONES 7–9

Skimmia × confusa 'Kew Green'

The first time I met with this shrub was at Borde Hill near Haywards Heath in Sussex. It was one of several different skimmias growing in what once was the most extensive private collection of woody plants in Britain. The collection was established earlier this century by Colonel Stephenson Clarke, regarded by no less an authority than the late Sir Harold Hillier as the greatest 'all round' amateur gardener of the twentieth century.

The skimmias were mainly concentrated in borders flanking the main drive to the house and 'Kew Green' was well represented with at least one large grouping. It is a superb evergreen easily recognised among other skimmias, especially those of the *Skimmia japonica* alliance, by its dense almost perfect domes of rich green foliage, each branch supporting a dense terminal head of pale green flower buds conspicuous throughout winter. These open in mid spring to creamy white with a faint cool hint of green and with contrasting orange anthers. They also possess a fine fragrance contrasting with the pointed leaves which, when bruised or crushed, have a strong sharp aroma.

It is a vigorous plant reaching on average 1m x 1.7m (3ft x 5ft) but capable of more when in a good soil and situation. It enjoys sun or half-shade in an acid or alkaline soil so long as there is sufficient moisture during summer. Like all skimmias it is a gross feeder and the best specimens are found in soils containing plenty of humus. In poor dry soils it is likely to suffer from red spider mite during prolonged dry weather.

The name 'Kew Green' was given to this plant only comparatively recently. Previously it was grown wrongly as *Skimmia laureola* 'male form' and still is in some quarters. Indeed, it is under this name that it was grown at Borde Hill and only in the last few years has

Skimmia × confusa
(**Family:** Rutaceae)
Pronunciation: *skim*-ee-a
Meaning: from the Japanese name *Miyami-Shikimi*
Pronunciation: kon-*few*-sa
Meaning: confused (with other kinds).

its true status been determined. This was decided at the Royal Botanic Gardens Kew by the botanist Nigel Taylor who, having satisfied himself that this plant was the result of a hybrid (*Skimmia anquetilia* × *S. japonica*) and in view of the confusion surrounding it in cultivation, christened it appropriately, *Skimmia* × *confusa*. It is a male form and therefore bears no fruit but there is a taller growing female cultivar of the same hybrid known as *S.* × *confusa* 'Isabella', a free-flowering shrub with bright red berries for which 'Kew Green' is the natural partner.

No one seems to know when and where the plant now known as 'Kew Green' originated, although given that *S. japonica* is Japanese and *S. anquetilia* comes from the western Himalaya it obviously arose somewhere in cultivation. The true *S. laureola*, by the way, has only recently been introduced to cultivation from east Nepal and south-west China. It differs most strikingly from other skimmias in its shining black berries. *S.* × *confusa* 'Kew Green' is without doubt one of the best low growing hardy evergreens for the garden and is most impressive with its large conical flower-heads in spring. It is easily propagated by cuttings in late summer and autumn.

Telopea truncata

One of the few disappointments I suffered during my visit to Tasmania in 1988 was not seeing the Tasmanian waratah *Telopea truncata* in flower. The reason, of course, is simple for although I travelled into the mountains where this shrub grows and actually saw its leafy stems, I was there at the wrong time, in January and February – the Tasmanian summer – whereas the waratah is a spring-flowering shrub which in Tasmania means November into December. It was nevertheless an exciting experience seeing this shrub for the first time in the wild on Mount Wellington which rises 1,270m (4,166ft) above the capital Hobart. Here, the waratah is found in the subalpine zone often as an understorey to the Tasmanian snow gum – *Eucalyptus coccifera* – the two making a handsome partnership when the former is in bloom.

One of only four species – all of them Australian – *T. truncata* is endemic to Tasmania, that is, it is found nowhere else in a wild state. It is not recorded when it was first introduced into cultivation in Britain, probably during the last century, but the most successful introduction was that made by the plant collector Harold Comber from his 1929/30 expedition. Its success was such that only four years later flowering material was being shown from a Plymouth garden to the Royal Horticultural Society who gave it an Award of Merit and four years after that similar material from Exbury Gardens in Hampshire was awarded a First Class Certificate.

Seeing this shrub flowering in the wild is one thing, seeing it flowering in cultivation is quite another for its rich crimson or scarlet red flowers are so curious and exotic when compared with

Telopea truncata
(**Family:** Proteaceae)
Pronunciation: tay-*lō*-pee-a
Meaning: from the Greek *telopos* (seen from afar) referring to the showy flowers
Pronunciation: trung-*kah*-ta
Meaning: abruptly cut off (the tips of the seed wings).

west and in warm pockets elsewhere. Even then it is best grown against a warm sheltering wall where, once established and given the support of wires or a similar framework, it is capable of reaching 2–3m (6–10ft) or twice this in optimum conditions.

I have a plant of this lovely shrub on the south-facing wall of my Hampshire home which I put out in 1984. It has survived two winters during which -10°C (15°F) was recorded on a number of nights and although some leaf loss and shoot damage occurred it continues to grow and flower its heart out. Its wiry arching or pendulous stems do need supporting and an alternative to wires is to train it through another, hardier wall shrub; a small leaved ceanothus or similar. The stems are fragile and easily broken. It makes a handsome plant for the conservatory and is best given the support of a wire frame to prevent an untidy habit. It enjoys a well-drained acid to alkaline soil so long as extremes are avoided: too rich a soil and growth is lush and more prone to frost damage. Propagation is by cuttings in summer or by seed when available.

Abelia floribunda
(Family: Caprifoliaceae)
Pronunciation: a-*bel*-ee-a
Meaning: after Dr Clarke Abel (1780–1826) who introduced *A. chinensis*
Pronunciation: flō-ri-*bun*-da
Meaning: free flowering.

Abutilon vitifolium 'Tennant's White'

For speed of growth and freedom of flowering few shrubs can beat *Abutilon vitifolium* and its hybrids. It is a native of Chile and was first recorded in European cultivation growing in a greenhouse in the Dublin garden of Capt. Edward Cottingham, a keen amateur. He is said to have obtained seeds direct from Chile in 1836. Four years later he exhibited flowering material before the council of the Royal Horticultural Society of Ireland who awarded him the Society's Gold Medal. He distributed seeds of his plant to other gardens, including that of the Horticultural Society of London (now the RHS) in 1839 and after a second introduction was made by William Lobb for Messrs Veitch of Exeter in 1844 it became widely grown.

A. vitifolium is vigorous and soft-wooded, reaching 3–5m (10–16ft) high, up to twice this in warm sheltered situations in mild areas where it often assumes a tree-like habit. Its long-stalked, evergreen, maple-like leaves, 10–15cm (4–6in) long, are clothed, like the young shoots, with a dense grey woolly felt which is most conspicuous on the young growths. The lavender blue or mauve-blue flowers are cup-shaped and slightly nodding at first, opening flat later like those of a fragile rose. They are borne several together on a long woolly stalk from the leaf axils on the previous year's growth appearing for several weeks from late spring into early summer and intermittently through summer.

Grown from seed, which is abundantly produced, the flowers of seedlings are variable in size and colour and several selections have been named of which 'Veronica Tennant' is undoubtedly the best with its large pale lavender flowers 7.5cm (3in) or more across. There is a fine white version of this known as 'Tennant's White' which arose as a seedling of 'Veronica Tennant'. When

I first joined Hilliers Nurseries in 1962 there was considerable excitement among the more experienced staff about an Abutilon species recently received which was reported to have darker flowers. This duly flowered and although they were somewhat smaller than those of *A. vitifolium* they were indeed a lovely violet-blue with a darker eye and contrasting boss of yellow stamens. It also differed from the other in its smaller, greener, less densely hairy leaves. We heard later that its name was *Abutilon ochsenii* and that it had been introduced to England in about 1957 by that fine gardener the late E.B. Anderson. He had been sent seed from a plant growing in the garden of Senhora Margharita Manns who had in turn collected it in the wild in Valdivia, Chile. A young plant in the Hillier Arboretum had survived the severe winter of 1962/63 and appeared, if anything, to be hardier than *A. vitifolium*.

It was not long before the possibilities of crossing the above two species began to occupy the thoughts of the Hillier propagators and in 1967 this was duly carried out by Peter Dummer using *A. vitifolium* 'Veronica Tennant' as the mother parent. Seedlings were produced one of which was eventually selected for its vigour and named 'Jermyns' after the home of the late Sir Harold Hillier where the seedlings were grown and assessed. It is intermediate in character between the parents; the leaves tending towards *A. ochsenii*, the flowers also but slightly larger and without the dark eye.

Meanwhile, the cross occurred accidentally in several other gardens in the south of England including Highdown near Worthing in Sussex, home of the late Sir Frederick Stern where *A. ochsenii* as well as *A. vitifolium* in both lavender- and white-flowered forms were being grown. Seed of the white form had been sent by Sir Frederick to the seedsmen Thompson and Morgan of Ipswich and a packet of this was purchased by, among others, the late Geoffrey Gorer of Sunte House, Haywards Heath, Sussex. Among the resultant seedlings were several intermediate in character between the parents. It was on these seedlings that Mr C.D. Brickell, then director of the Royal Horticultural Society's Garden at Wisley, based the name *Abutilon* × *suntense* which covers all such hybrids, hence the name *A.* × *suntense* 'Jermyns' and *A.* × *suntense* 'Sunte House'. These hybrids have proven hardier than either parent and although like them relatively short lived, they give excellent value for money with clouds of richly coloured flowers from late spring through early summer. There are also white-flowered seedlings available.

All the hybrids are vigorous and will attain 3–5m (10–16ft) eventually. They flower and seed so freely, however, that after ten years or less they are often exhausted and begin to deteriorate. They can be pruned hard if necessary but it is probably better to replace them with young plants raised from cuttings in late summer or from seed which will produce seedlings varying in depth of flower colour. They love a sunny sheltered position and are best grown in a well-drained none too rich soil; otherwise, they will develop too fast and furiously. As with *A. vitifolium*, the hybrids are not suitable for consistently cold areas, while even in mild areas wet summers result in soft unripened shoots which are easy prey to frost.

Abutilon vitifolium
(**Family:** Malvaceae)
Pronunciation: a-*bew*-ti-lon
Meaning: from the Arabic name for a similar plant
Pronunciation: vee-ti-*fo*-lee-um
Meaning: with leaves like a vine (*vitis*).

Abutilon vitifolium 'Tennant's White'
- HARDY IN MILD AREAS, BUT MAY NEED PROTECTION ELSEWHERE
- SUN
- MOST WELL-DRAINED SOILS
- EVERGREEN
- ZONES 8–10

Below: *Azara serrata*
- HARDY IN MILD AREAS, BUT MAY NEED PROTECTION ELSEWHERE
- SUN OR HALF-SHADE
- LIME-FREE SOIL
- EVERGREEN
- ZONES 8–10

Azara serrata

The forests of Chile are full of ornamental evergreens – trees and shrubs – among which the azaras are noted for their clusters or racemes of yellow flowers in spring or summer. Of the species most usually encountered in cultivation *Azara microphylla* is a distinctive tree and strictly outside the scope of this book, although it is the hardiest of the genus and is often seen as a large bush against a sheltering but not necessarily sunny wall. Its arching branches are produced in flattened twiggy sprays, densely clothed with small, toothed, dark green leaves whilst the clusters of tiny yellow flowers on the undersides of the shoots fill the air around in late winter or early spring with a delightful vanilla-like fragrance.

Azara serrata by contrast is summer flowering and densely bushy in habit reaching 3m (10ft) and as much across with little difficulty. It is capable of twice this in the wild or in a mild sheltered location. Its leaves are oval, to 4cm (1 1/2in) long, toothed and a glossy bright green above. Like all azaras, its tiny flowers are without petals, the clusters of yellow stamens being the attraction. In this species they are crowded together in rounded heads which are held above the foliage on slender stalks. After a warm summer these are followed by small whitish fruits the size of a peppercorn.

A. serrata is a cheerful evergreen only suitable, however, for milder areas and warm pockets. It is best grown against a warm sheltering wall and should it suffer frost damage it can safely be pruned in late spring to encourage strong new growth. It will grow in sun or half-shade *A. serrata* can be propagated by cuttings in late summer or by seed when available.

Azara serrata
(**Family:** Flacourtiaceae)
Pronunciation: a-*zah*-ra
Meaning: after J.N. Azara (1731–1804), a Spanish scientist
Pronunciation: se-*rah*-ta
Meaning: saw-toothed (the leaves).

Buddleja davidii 'Dartmoor'

The common buddleja or butterfly bush has long been among the most popular of garden shrubs, partly because of its ease of cultivation and more tellingly because of its floriferous habit. It can be grown easily and is tolerant of any condition other than a bog. I remember it from my boyhood days in Bolton in the late 1940s and early 1950s when it was grown in almost every garden, a colourful antidote to the pollution, then a fact of everyday life in the South Lancashire Industrial belt. Beyond the gardens, it was sometimes found in waste places in towns and on railway embankments and sidings where its tiny parachuted seeds found the well-drained rubble or cinders ideal conditions for successful germination. I can even remember it sprouting from walls where mortar was crumbling and, once, 12m (40ft) up on a derelict chimney. This pattern could be repeated in many areas of the country and I was not at all surprised when I first arrived in Winchester in the early 1960s to find it equally well established on the ancient walls of this city. So common is this shrub and so adaptable is it to a variety of situations that I began to ponder on its occurrence and habit in the wild.

Buddleja davidii is native to central and west China and was first discovered in Mupin (now Baoxing) in Sichuan by the French missionary, Armand David, in 1869. Subsequently, it was found and collected by several travellers and plant hunters including the Russians but it was not until the seed collections of E.H. Wilson reached the West, in the first decade of the present century, that *B. davidii*, as we now know it in gardens, became established. In

Buddleja davidii 'Dartmoor'

- HARDY
- SUN
- MOST SOILS
- ZONES 6–9

the wild it grows in rocks and shingle on stream and river banks as well as on cliffs and in scrub. On many occasions in the mountains of western Sichuan I have seen it often crowding ravines and gullies. However, most of the flowers I have seen in the wild have been a washy purple or lilac and of little, if any, garden merit. The importance of Wilson's introductions lay in the fact that several highly ornamental forms with flowers in larger panicles and more richly coloured were included providing the basis for many of the splendid cultivars available today.

Most cultivars are vigorous, ultimately large shrubs to 5m (16ft) high and wide if left unpruned, flowering on the current year's shoots from mid summer through to early or mid autumn. Pruning, by the way, encourages an annual crop of stronger shoots bearing larger leaves and, more importantly, larger flower heads. To achieve this the old shoots should be removed to within a bud or two of their base in late winter or early spring. Among the wide variety of cultivars available 'Dartmoor' is one of my favourites. It is of recent introduction having apparently been found by a retired gardener Mr Hayles in around 1971 while on holiday in Devon.

According to one story, Mr Hayles was walking with his wife on

Buddleja davidii
(**Family:** Loganiaceae)
Pronunciation: bŭd-*lee*-a
Meaning: after the Rev. Adam Buddle (1660-1715). Linnaeus, when naming this genus deliberately chose the above spelling (with a j instead of an i)
Pronunciation: dă-*vid*-ee-ee
Meaning: after Père David, the French missionary who first discovered it.

a part of Dartmoor above Yelverton when he spotted the buddleja naturalised in a nearby, yet inaccessible hollow. So impressed was he by its flowers that with his wife hanging onto his coat-tails he managed to obtain cuttings which on his return home he succeeded in rooting. Once established in cultivation, 'Dartmoor', as it was now christened, amply repaid its finder's confidence by earning an Award of Merit from the Royal Horticultural Society in 1973, capturing the attention and admiration of all who saw it.

It differs so markedly from all others in its inflorescence which instead of being a long tapering panicle is shorter and stubbier but with a number of side branches also flowering to produce an appearance reminiscent of a lilac. In colour the flowers are a rich magenta and in common with others of its clan are very popular with butterflies, bees and other nectar-seeking insects. The flowers of *B. davidii* and its cultivars, by the way, possess a rich fruity fragrance that reminds me of stewed blackberries. This is more obvious when your nose is held close to the flower.

Other cultivars worth growing include 'Royal Red' raised by Messrs Good and Reese and introduced in 1941 with flowers of a rich purplish red (Award of Merit 1950). There are also two variegated sports of this, 'Royal Red Variegated' and the lower growing and superior 'Harlequin'. In both, the leaves are irregularly margined creamy white. 'Black Knight' has flowers of a deep violet, the darkest of any buddleja and was raised by the Dutch firm of Ruys in 1959. Also from Holland is 'Pink Delight' introduced by the Boskoop Research Station in 1986. This is the result of a multiple hybrid involving the lilac-pink 'Fascinating', the white 'Nanhoensis Alba' and the mauve-blue 'West Hill', itself a hybrid between *B. davidii* and the more tender *B. fallowiana*. *Buddleja* 'Pink Delight' is an outstanding shrub producing noticeably larger dense conical panicles of a bright pink. Finally, 'White Profusion' is arguably the best of several whites. All these buddlejas are best propagated from cuttings in summer. Seed, whilst abundantly produced and easy to germinate, gives somewhat variable results – in other words the good, the bad and the ugly.

Carpenteria californica

The so-called bush anemone *Carpenteria californica* is one of a number of spectacular flowering shrubs which have reached our gardens from California. It is an evergreen shrub with several main stems, erect at first, later spreading widely when it can become rather open and straggling. It is capable of reaching from 2–3m (6–10ft), even higher against a wall, and as much through and therefore needs plenty of space to accommodate its potential spread. The grey bark of the older stem peels away in long strips while the lance-shaped leaves in pairs are dark green above and pale or glaucous beneath. These are a suitable foil for the fragrant white,

Carpenteria californica
(**Family:** Philadelphaceae)
Pronunciation: kar-pen-*te*-ree-a
Meaning: after Prof. William M. Carpenter, Louisiana physician
Pronunciation: kăl-i-*for*-ni-ka
Meaning: of California.

golden-stamened flowers which are borne in terminal clusters any time from late spring to mid summer and intermittently into late summer. A plant in full bloom is a show-stopper, especially in the cultivar 'Ladham's Variety' which has flowers up to 8cm (3in) in diameter with overlapping petals. This selection was introduced to commerce some time before 1924 by Messrs Ladham, nurserymen of Southampton. In 1924 it received an Award of Merit from the Royal Horticultural Society to be followed sometime later in 1985 by a First Class Certificate.

In the wild, *C. californica* has a restricted distribution in Fresno County between the San Joaquin and Kings rivers where it is mainly found on thin, poor, sharply drained soils on gentle slopes in chaparral country. It was first discovered in 1845 by Captain (later Major-General) John Charles Fremont (1830–90), known as 'Pathfinder Fremont', a geographer and scientist in the south-western United States. The circumstances of its discovery are perhaps worth recounting here.

It was made while Captain Fremont was attempting to return eastwards across the Sierra Nevada to rejoin the remainder of his previously divided party. According to Philip McMillan Browse in a recent article, Fremont intended to traverse the range via the head of the San Joaquin river but he became lost in virtually uncharted country (having mistaken the Kings river for the Kern and was

Carpenteria californica
- HARDY IN WARM AREAS
- SUN
- WELL-DRAINED SOIL
- EVERGREEN
- ZONES 8–10

forced to turn back by bad weather and the impassable terrain. Subsequent attempts to relocate the plant proved unsuccessful as Fremont's route was unknown and was still debated, even he was puzzled by his failure and was unable to throw any light on it. It remained a mystery until 1875 when one Gustav Eisen struck lucky returning with a specimen he had picked at a place called Grapevine Spring. According to D.C. Peattie in his book, *A Natural History of Western Trees*, first published in 1950, Fremont proved an incompetent soldier and governor since he seldom found a trail ir all the West not already known to traders, trappers and Indians. He was, however, an accomplished topographer and linguist.

Carpenteria enjoys in cultivation a sunny situation and a well-drained soil and given this it is reasonably hardy in all but the coldest areas. Its young growths in any garden, however, are susceptible to late spring frosts unless afforded adequate protection. Its tendency to become straggly with age can be controlled by hard pruning, even into the old wood, in summer after the main flush of flowering.

Propagation is by seed, although seedlings are variable in flower quality and habit, and when buying it is wise to confirm that the plant is of a 'good' form. Cuttings in early summer is the best means of reproducing selected forms. Several selections noted for their quality of habit or flower have been made available recently in the USA and when these are generally available they should be well worth trying.

Cistus × aguilari 'Maculatus'

The Cistus species and hybrids in British cultivation fall into two categories; those that are relatively hardy and those that are not. *Cistus* × *aguilari* regretfully belongs to the latter. It is such a spectacular shrub, however, especially in its form 'Maculatus' that it is well worth trying in warmer areas and sheltered pockets. It is a hybrid between *Cistus ladanifer* and *Cistus populifolius*, found with its parents in the wild in south-west Europe (the Iberian Peninsula) and across the water, in Morocco.

It was first introduced into British cultivation from southern Spain by Sir Oscar Warburg (1876–1937) who made a special study of *Cistus* as well as *Quercus* and *Sorbus*. His plant, which probably had *C. populifolius* var. *lasiocalyx* as one parent, makes a fairly dense evergreen shrub of vigorous growth to 2m (6ft) with lance-shaped bright green wavy edged leaves to 10cm (4in) long. The flowers in early and mid summer are like single white roses to 10cm (4in) across with a central boss of golden stamens. In 'Maculatus' the petals have a deep crimson stain near the base which gives the flower a striking dark-eyed look.

The leaves too are different in that they are decidedly sticky (gummy) as in the gum cistus *C. ladanifer* which suggests that it is the result of a back-cross, *C.* × *aguilari* × *C. ladanifer*. It arose

Cistus* × *aguilari
'Maculatus'
(**Family:** Cistaceae)
Pronunciation: *kis*-tus usually pronounced *sis*-tus
Meaning: from the Greek name for these plants
Pronunciation: a-gwi-*lah*-ree
Meaning: of Aguilar in southern Spain
Pronunciation: mă-kew-*lah*-tus
Meaning: spotted (the petals).

Cistus × *aquilari* 'Maculatus'

- HARDY IN MILD AREAS
- SUN
- WELL-DRAINED PREFERABLY LIME-FREE SOILS
- EVERGREEN
- ZONES 8–10

in the garden of Sir Oscar Warburg and was the recipient of an Award of Merit from the Royal Horticultural Society in 1936. Other cistus hybrids worth considering are *Cistus* 'Anne Palmer' and *Cistus* 'Peggy Sammons' both of which are pink flowered. The former, named after Lady Anne Palmer previously of Rosemoor, Devon was raised at Benenden, Kent by Captain Collingwood Ingram some time before 1960 as a cross between *Cistus crispus* and *Cistus* 'Paladin' (*pallinhae* × *ladanifer*). It is an upright shrub to 2m (6ft) with narrow, green wavy margined leaves and flowers 5–7.5cm (2–3in) across in early and mid summer. It received an Award of Merit from the RHS in 1960 the same year in which its raiser was awarded the Reginald Cory Memorial Cup for the best deliberate hybrid shown to the Society that year.

'Peggy Sammons' is more bushy than 'Anne Palmer', growing to 2m (6ft) with oval, grey-green downy leaves and pale pink flowers 5cm (2in) or more across in early and mid summer. It is the result of a deliberate cross between *Cistus albidus* (mother parent) and *Cistus laurifolius* made by Mr J.E. Sammons of Walsall, Staffordshire in 1956 and named after his wife. Both are hardier than *Cistus* × *aguilarii* though less so than *Cistus* × *corbariensis* – a hybrid between *Cistus populifolius* and *C. salviifolius*. For several years, until it grew too large for its position, a plant of this cistus grew in a narrow bed on my terrace. It was a well-drained position in full sun and it grew into a dense mounded bush up to 1m (3ft) high, spreading to twice this. It was pleasant enough throughout the year with its downy green wavy edged leaves and in June it was covered with

yellow-eyed white flowers slightly less than 4cm ($1^1/2$in) across. Only once was it slightly damaged during one of the three severe winters when temperatures of −10°C (15°F) were experienced but it completely recovered the following spring. It is undoubtedly one of the hardiest cistus in cultivation but needs plenty of elbow-room if it is to reach its full potential.

All cistus are evergreen and require a warm sunny, well-drained situation to do their best. Plants grown in rich soils with plenty of moisture in summer wax fat and lush and are rarely as long lived, although no cistus survives to a great age. They are especially successful in coastal gardens in milder regions. Their flowers have a comparatively brief life opening in the morning, their petals generally shed by the end of the day. Fortunately, they are produced in such quantity that there are plenty to replace those that fall!

Cistus can be clipped lightly to remove damaged growth or, in the taller kinds, their shoots can be shortened to encourage a more compact bushier habit. This is best done when they are still small. Never prune into the old wood as cistus rarely break again and specimens on the wane are best replaced by young plants overwintered from cuttings taken in summer. Cistus produce plenty of seed and often self-sown seedlings can be found in the vicinity of the parent. While raising cistus from seed can bring a few surprises, the selected forms and hybrids are best propagated vegetatively. They resent disturbance hence their being grown by nurserymen in containers. Once planted they are best left well alone.

Deutzia × elegantissima 'Rosealind'

Pierre Louis Victor Lemoine (1823–1911) was a remarkable French nurseryman whose name, and that of his son, Emile (1862–1943) who succeeded him, will always be remembered by gardeners for the many lovely woody plant hybrids they bred at their nursery at Nancy in the province of Lorraine. These included lilacs, philadelphus, weigela and deutzia, many of which are still popular today.

Among the deutzias presently in cultivation there are over a dozen hybrids raised by Lemoine – these include *Deutzia × carnea*, *Deutzia × rosea*, *Deutzia × kalmiiflora*, *Deutzia × magnifica*, *Deutzia × maliflora*, *Deutzia × hybrida*, *Deutzia × candelabra*, *Deutzia × elegantissima* and, of course, *Deutzia × lemoinei*. One of the loveliest of these is *D. × elegantissima* which Lemoine believed to be a variety of the Chinese *Deutzia discolor*. It has since proved to be a hybrid between this species and the Japanese *Deutzia sieboldiana*. The latter was introduced to European cultivation in 1890, 11 years before *D. discolor* and both were represented in the extensive collections in the Lemoine nursery.

In habit *D. × elegantissima* is fairly erect to 1.7m or 2m (5 or 6ft) with sharply pointed and toothed leaves and loose erect clusters of five-petalled flowers 2cm (1in) across which are rose-pink in bud

Opposite: ***Deutzia × elegantissima* 'Rosealind'**

- HARDY
- SUN
- MOST SOILS
- ZONES 5–9

opening white flushed rose, darker on the outside. They are freely borne along the shoots of the previous year in June. Even better than the original, however, is *D.* × *elegantissima* 'Rosealind' which was raised by the Slieve Donard Nursery of Newcastle, Co. Down in the 1930s and named after the proprietor Leslie Slinger's eldest daughter. According to the late Harry Bryce, then Head Propagator, he was taking cuttings from *D.* × *elegantissima* in a nursery border when he noticed a sporting shoot with a darker flower. He took a cutting of the sport and from this all the others originated. It is a smaller shrub to 1.7m (5ft), while the flowers are a deep carmine pink flooding the branches in June. If I had to choose just one deutzia for my garden it would be this. It is quite hardy and amenable growing on most, preferably fertile, soils even those above chalk so long as moisture is available during summer. Old plants can become rather dense and crowded in which event the older stems and branches should be pruned to the base after the flowers have faded. It can be propagated by cuttings in summer.

Considered one of the finest of the white flowering wild deutzias is *Deutzia setchuenensis* var. *corymbiflora*, whose name simply means the deutzia from Szetchuan (now Sichuan), with flowers in corymbs (branched clusters). It is not the most satisfactory deutzia in wetter or colder areas as it benefits from a good summer ripening, yet its substantial clusters of pure white star-like flowers through early and mid summer on a bush up to 2m (6ft) high are a sight for sore eyes. For many years in the 1960s and 1970s a fine specimen grew on the chalk soil of the Hillier West Hill Nursery in Winchester where its sunny well-drained position seemed to suit it well.

Deutzia* × *elegantissima
(**Family:** Philadelphaceae)
Pronunciation: *doytz*-ee-a
Meaning: after Johann van der Deutz (1743–88), a patron of the botanist Carl Peter Thunberg
Pronunciation: ay-le-gan-*tis*-i-ma
Meaning: most elegant.

Fremontodendron 'California Glory'

By all accounts John Charles Fremont was a colourful character in the mould of a '*Boy's Own* Paper' hero, as the late Alice Coates once remarked. His career as an officer in the US Corps of Topographical Engineers took him to the rank of Major-General and involved him in a great deal of travel in little known terrain. He was a geographer and topographer by profession but was also trained as a scientist and made numerous botanical collections and observations. His collections were of dried specimens for the herbarium rather than living plants and included about 16 new species and two new genera one of which was *Fremontodendron* or *Fremontia* as it was originally named. Unfortunately, Torrey, the author of the name *Fremontia*, had already used it for another quite different plant hence the later correct name *Fremontodendron*.

Fremont made four notable journeys into south-west United States from east to west and it was during one of these in 1846 that he found *Fremontodendron californicum*, the species most usually seen in cultivation. It was introduced to Britain soon after and first flowered in the Horticultural Society's old garden at Chiswick in

Fremontodendron
'California Glory'

- HARDY IN MILD AREAS, BUT MAY NEED PROTECTION ELSEWHERE
- SUN
- WELL-DRAINED PREFERABLY LIME-FREE SOILS
- EVERGREEN
- ZONES 8–10

1854. This plant was later sold for the princely sum of £40 but died soon after. It was re-introduced, however, by the Veitch collector William Lobb in 1853 and has been in cultivation ever since. Given its frost tender nature it is only suitable for growing outdoors in warmer areas and even there it is perhaps best grown against a sunny sheltering wall or fence to receive the maximum amount of sunlight and warmth.

It is not long lived in cultivation, 10 to 20 years or so on average, but amply repays its keep with a summer-long display of rich golden yellow flowers, cup-shaped at first later flattening, borne singly on short leafy spurs on the current year's growth. Curiously, there are no petals, their role being taken by the enlarged calyx. Each lobe has at its base (inside) a small pit filled with white hairs. There is no scent but the sheer brilliance of the flowers which often become orange or reddish yellow on the outside with age, more than compensates and their continuous appearance from late spring to mid or late summer makes this one of the most reliable of all shrubs for summer colour. In mild areas it can be grown as a free-standing shrub or small tree of 5–6m (16–20ft), more in a sheltered site. However, its vigorous growth is often too much for its root system to support and sometimes results in collapse, hence its suitability for a high wall which it will soon top. Spread is not generally equal to height but it does nevertheless require plenty of elbow-room.

The leaves are evergreen except in a cold winter and three-lobed, green above and covered beneath, like the young shoots, with a dense pelt of golden brown hairs which come adrift when handled and can cause pain if they get into your eyes. Indeed, if it is necessary to prune this plant or any of its hybrids it would be wise to wear a mask and gloves for the hairs are like golden asbestos and should not be inhaled. Pruning can be quite severe – into the old wood if necessary to rejuvenate an old or leggy specimen – and is best done immediately after flowering sometime in late summer.

In the wild *F. californicum* and its varieties are found on the lower western slopes of the Sierra Nevada in California from Shasta County southwards and in various parts of the coastal ranges and Arizona. A second species *F. mexicanum* is native to the Mexican State of Baja California extending north just across the US border into San Diego County. It differs from *F. californicum* in, among other things, the flowers being produced directly on the main branchlets rather than on side spurs. It is grown and is available in Britain but by far the most commonly planted member of this genus here is a hybrid between the two species, namely 'California Glory' raised in 1952 on the old site of the Rancho Santa Ana Botanic Garden in Orange County, California. I have a plant of this hybrid on the south wall of my house in Hampshire where it has attained 7m (25ft) in eight years. The flowers are 5–6cm (2–2½in) across and lemon yellow becoming darker and red-stained on the outside with age. They are produced continuously with the growing shoots from late spring through to early autumn providing one of the longest displays of continuous flowering that I know of. Its branching is fairly open and I have used my plant as a vehicle for several slender-stemmed climbers including the white flowered potato vine *Solanum jasminoides* 'Album'. In October 1989 this specimen was wrenched from its supports during a gale and I returned from a weekend visit to find it lying on the ground. Fortunately, not all its roots had been broken and after pruning it severely I raised it back to the wall securing it even more firmly than before. Its resurrection was shortlived, however. After flowering prodigiously in the summer of 1990 it again fell foul of a fierce wind on Christmas Day and reluctantly I decided to cut it down to the base.

Fremontodendrons should be grown in well-drained even poor soils otherwise they wax too fat and invite trouble from frost or wind. Nor do they like excess wet which is a common cause of their early demise. Being bad transplanters they are sold by nurserymen in containers and once planted are best left well alone. They can be propagated by seed, while selected forms including 'California Glory' should be propagated by cuttings in late autumn or winter.

Fremontodendron
(**Family:** Sterculiaceae)
Pronunciation: fray-mont-ō-*den*-dron
Meaning: *Fremont* after Major-General J.C. Fremont (1813–90), American surveyor and explorer, and *dendron*, Greek name for a tree.

Fuchsia 'Mrs Popple'

Fuchsia 'Mrs Popple'
- HARDY
- SUN
- MOST SOILS
- ZONES 8–10

Anyone who has travelled through the west of Ireland in summer or early autumn will be familiar with the fuchsia which is such a common inhabitant of cottage gardens there. In some places as in Co. Kerry it has been extensively planted as a country hedge and is so established in places that a visitor might well believe it to be a native plant. This particular fuchsia, which is a robust grower with showers of small pendulous crimson and purple flowers, is *Fuchsia magellanica*, a native of temperate South America – mainly in southern Chile and Tierra del Fuego where it grows in the Nothofagus forest and along the coast in the Drimys-Nothofagus forest – where its flowers are pollinated by humming bees. According to Dr Charles Nelson of the National Botanic Gardens, Dublin, the establishment of *F. magellanica* as a garden plant in western Ireland dates back at least to the first half of the nineteenth century. The first recorded plant in Ireland, however, was already growing in the Belfast garden of John Templeton in the 1790s.

In the wild, this species is commonly found forming thickets along streamsides and in marshy places, often with *Berberis darwinii*, and it is not so surprising therefore that it should find itself a home from home in the ditches of Cork and Kerry. There are in addition several varieties of *F. magellanica* in cultivation such as *gracilis* and *molinae* (alba), the latter with white and pale lilac rose flowers. There are also

Fuchsia
(**Family:** Onagraceae)
Pronunciation: *fuks*–ee-a
Meaning: after Leonhart Fuchs (1501–66), a German physician and herbalist.

at least two variegated cultivars of which 'Versicolor', with silvery grey and cream leaves flushed crimson purple when young, is the most often seen. Sadly, this has an unfortunate habit of reverting to the green-leaved var. *gracilis*. In the last 10–20 years, however, a wide variety of hardier hybrids have found their way into our gardens, many of them originally raised as pot plants for glasshouses.

In mild areas these hybrids are typically deciduous shrubs but in colder areas or in severe winters elsewhere their top growth is killed and they behave almost as herbaceous perennials. Even when the top growth remains intact, these hybrids are perhaps best hard pruned to within a few buds of the base in early spring to encourage new growth. Flowers are borne on the current season's shoots so you are losing nothing by this treatment. All these hybrids flower continuously over a long period through summer into autumn often until the first hard frosts. They are among the most colourful, prodigious flowering and reliable of all shrubs for the garden and, as such, excellent value for money. The flowers normally have spreading or recurved sepals and a cup-shaped skirt of petals of a different colour. In some cultivars they are double.

One of my favourites is 'Mrs Popple', a vigorous bushy shrub up to 1.2m (4ft) high and wide, the flowers with soft crimson-scarlet tube and sepals and violet-blue ageing to crimson purple petals. I have several plants in my garden which I prune to the base each winter, the shoots crowding back again in spring and summer to provide a regular display of substantial flowers over a very long period. It is an old cultivar introduced by the British firm of Messrs Elliot in 1899. It received an Award of Merit from the Royal Horticultural Society in 1934 and a First Class Certificate from the same source after Trial at Wisley in 1965.

'Madame Cornelissen' is an even older hybrid dating back to 1860. A bushy shrub to 1m (3ft) with elegant foliage and slightly smaller single to semi-double flowers with crimson tube and sepals and white petals with cerise veins – a charming contrast. It is fully deserving of the First Class Certificate awarded it by the RHS in 1978. It was raised and introduced to commerce by the Belgian nursery Cornelissen in 1860.

'Chillerton Beauty' is rather spreading in habit but capable of 1.2m (4ft) in height, the flowers with tube and sepals a pale rose, flushed deeper rose and with violet petals. It was raised in Britain by Bass and introduced to commerce in 1847. 'Margaret', meanwhile, is a vigorous cultivar of vase-shaped habit 1.3m to 1.7m (4–5ft) in height, the semi-double flowers with scarlet tube and sepals and spreading petals of bluish-violet with white flares at the base. It was raised by the late W.P. Wood of Berrington, Hertfordshire, by crossing the cultivar 'Heritage' with *F. magellanica* var. *molinae* and received an Award of Merit from the RHS in 1965. It was introduced to commerce in either 1937 or 1946.

'Alice Hoffman' is a German-raised cultivar introduced by Klese in 1911. It is of compact upright habit to 1m (3ft) with dark bronze-green young foliage and semi-double flowers in which the tube and sepals are rose while the petals are white with rose veins. Smallest of all are 'Tom Thumb' and 'Lady Thumb' both of them recipients of the RHS First Class Certificate after Trial at Wisley, the former in 1962, the latter in 1978. 'Tom Thumb' is an old cultivar thought to have been introduced by Baudinat of Meaux, France as long ago as 1850. It is a neat little gem of upright, compact growth, very free flowering with carmine tube and sepals and mauve-purple petals. 'Lady Thumb' was raised by George Roe of Nottingham as a sport on 'Tom Thumb' and introduced to commerce in 1966. It is similar to the latter in habit but with semi-double flowers in which the tube and sepals are carmine and the petals white with pink veins. Both plants are excellent subjects for rock gardens, raised beds, narrow borders or for bedding.

A hardy cultivar of more recent appearance is 'Sealand Prince'. It was introduced by Bees Nurseries of Sealand, Cheshire, in 1967 having received an Award of Merit from the RHS after Trial at Wisley in 1965. It is bushy and upright in habit to 1m (3ft) or more, the flowers with light red tube and sepals and pale violet-purple petals maturing to reddish purple.

Finally, two coloured leaved cultivars which are hardy enough in warmer areas, but which are worth growing for summer effect in colder districts so long as they are brought under glass or cuttings are taken before winter. 'Genii' was introduced by Victor Reiter of San Francisco, USA, in 1951 and is a dwarf bushy shrub with light yellowish green leaves on red stems. The flowers have cerise tubes and sepals and rich violet petals maturing to dark rose. The best foliage colour is achieved on plants grown in full sun. 'Sharpitor' is a probable sport of *F. magellanica* var. *molinae* raised at the National Trust garden at Sharpitor in Devon in around 1974. It is a bushy shrub with very small pale mauve and pink flowers but its main attraction lies in its variegated leaves which are grey-green with an irregular creamy white margin.

All these fuchsias enjoy a fertile soil and a sunny position to give of their best. Those grown in colder areas can be either deep planted, i.e. with the base of the stems below the soil surface, or given a generous mulching of leaf mould, well-rotted manure or similar organic matter in autumn taking care to cover the crown. Even in mild districts, however, it is wise to root extra plants from cuttings taken in summer, overwintering them under glass.

Genista aetnensis

I am told, though I have never had the opportunity to see for myself, that the slopes of Mount Etna in Sicily are gilded in July with the flowering of a myriad brooms. The effect I am assured can be seen from some distance away. What wouldn't I give to see this spectacle, for the broom in question *Genista aetnensis* is one of the loveliest of its kind in gardens and has long been a particular favourite of mine. Commonly known as the Mount Etna broom it is amongst the most graceful of large shrubs with its long slender almost rush-like bright green branches which are pendulous at first virtually leafless and peppered in July with golden-yellow pea-flowers. These are smaller than those of the English broom (*Cytisus scoparius*) but so elegantly displayed that the effect is charming rather than stunning. It is a free-growing large but open-habited shrub capable of 6m (20ft) or more in time and as much across.

It can be trained to a single stem if preferred so long as training is begun when the plant is still small. Pruning should not be carried into the old wood as it rarely, if ever, sprouts anew nor should a plant once established be moved as it resents disturbance, hence the need for nurserymen to grow it in containers. Apart from Sicily it is also native to Sardinia. It is not too fussy about soil as long as it is well drained and, naturally, it prefers full sun. Otherwise, it is quite hardy and an excellent subject for the back of a border where its sparse habit creates an ever shifting dappled shade. It is also useful in the larger heather garden and makes a lovely specimen, where space permits, isolated in a lawn or terrace bed. Propagation is by seed or by cuttings in late summer. It was awarded a First Class Certificate by the Royal Horticultural Society in 1938.

Another large broom worth considering for the garden is *Genista tenera*, a native of Madeira and Tenerife, introduced to Britain from the last named by Kew collector Francis Masson on his way home from the Cape of Good Hope in 1777. It is of bushier habit than *G. aetnensis* therefore less graceful reaching eventually 4m (13ft) by as much across. It also blooms about a month earlier from early to mid summer, the bright yellow pea-flowers borne in short racemes along the spreading branches creating a cloud of gold from a distance. In its likes and dislikes it is similar to the other with the exception that it is tolerant of a reasonable amount of shade which makes it an excellent shrub beneath scattered trees. It is also free seeding to the point of naturalising if conditions permit. The typical plant, which was once known as *G. virgata*, is easily propagated from seed but in the selection 'Golden Showers' seed is not produced and propagation is normally with difficulty by cuttings in late summer. This selection is, if anything, even more free flowering and the flowers have a decided fragrance – a useful bonus.

Genista aetnensis
(**Family:** Leguminosae)
Pronunciation: ge-*nis*-ta
Meaning: the Latin name
Pronunciation: iet-*nen*-sis
Meaning: of Mt Etna, Sicily.

Genista aetnensis

- HARDY
- SUN
- MOST WELL-DRAINED SOILS
- ZONES 8–10

Grevillea juniperina
'Sulphurea'

- HARDY IN MILD AREAS, BUT MAY NEED PROTECTION ELSEWHERE SUN
- WELL-DRAINED LIME-FREE SOILS
- EVERGREEN
- ZONES 9–10

Grevillea juniperina 'Sulphurea'

There is something particularly satisfying about growing and flowering an Australian plant in one's garden and when that plant continues to flourish year after year despite the occasional cold winter it is a cause for celebration. So it is with *Grevillea juniperina* 'Sulphurea', previously known as *Grevillea sulphurea.*

G. juniperina is native to New South Wales where it is locally common in sandy or shaley soils, even approaching the western suburbs of Sydney. It is an erect shrub, spreading later, up to 2m (6ft) tall and as much across, the stems much branched and densely clothed with needle-like leaves up to 2.5cm (1in) long. The flowers are produced in clusters at the ends of short branchlets and individually are slenderly tubular with a deep slit down one side through which protrudes the style. In colour they vary from pink to yellow or red.

'Sulphurea' is a selected form with pale yellow flowers deeper in bud and with rich green foliage. It is not recorded when or by whom it was introduced into cultivation. It is not to the best of my knowledge cultivated in Australia although several other forms of *G. juniperina* are grown there including a prostrate yellow-flowered selection, which could be a useful introduction to Britain. *G. juniperina* 'Sulphurea' is only suitable for warmer areas. Even here it is best given a sunny sheltered position in a bed or border or against a warm sheltering wall. It thrives best in a lime-free soil that is well drained. It does not like too much shade or an ill-drained or cold, heavy clay soil. My specimen I planted in 1984 in a terrace bed with other Mediterranean plants. It has never suffered in winter, even when temperatures plummeted on several occasions to -10°C (15°F) and it flowers profusely in late spring and early summer. In fact, flowers are produced off and on through most of the year and in mild winters they are already opening in mid or late winter. It will take pruning, should shaping be necessary or when stems are broken by strong winds. It is one of the most cheerful looking evergreens in my garden and I cannot recommend it highly enough. It can be propagated by cuttings in late summer.

Grevillea juniperina
'Sulphurea'
(**Family:** Proteaceae)
Pronunciation: gre-*vil*-ee-a
Meaning: after Charles Francis Greville (1749–1809) one of the founders of the Horticultural Society of London, now the Royal Horticultural Society
Pronunciation: yoo-ni-pe-*ree*-na
Meaning: like Juniperus
Pronunciation: sul-*fu*-ree-a
Meaning: sulphur yellow (the flowers).

Grindelia chiloensis

Many years ago on one of my first visits to Kew Gardens I remember peeping through a gate into what was (and still is) the Alpine Department propagation area and seeing there a curious shrub. Its long stemmed bright yellow cornflowers intrigued me and I took a chance in sneaking in to look for a label. I duly located it and learned that this plant was *Grindelia chiloensis* a native of Argentina and neighbouring parts of Chile where it grows in dry places. It was originally introduced to Britain by H. Woolmer of Upper Tulse Hill, London, in about 1850 the seed having been sent to him by his son, who found it just above high water mark at a place called New Bay in Patagonia. It was, however, first described from a plant growing in the Ghent Botanic Garden, Belgium.

I have grown this plant in both my gardens, first on the chalk of Winchester and latterly on a clay soil near Southampton. It is an evergreen shrub to 1m (3ft) high and as much or more across with sticky erect shoots clothed with narrow often coarsely toothed grey-green leaves sticky to the touch. During summer from the ends of these shoots are produced single large yellow cornflowers which open continuously over a long period. A curious characteristic of the fat green flower bud is the white sticky gum which covers its top.

It is generally hardy, sometimes dying back in cold inland areas. It is tolerant of most soils so long as they are not too wet and it prefers a warm sunny situation. In cold areas it is best grown at the base of a warm wall. Propagation is by seeds or by cuttings in late summer.

Grindelia chiloensis
(**Family:** Compositae)
Pronunciation: grin-*del*-ee-a
Meaning: after David H. Grindel (1776–1836), a Russian botanist of German origin
Pronunciation: ki-lō-*en*-sis, usually pronounced chi-lō-*en*-sis
Meaning: after the island of Chiloe off the Chilean coast, where, incidentally, it does not occur.

× Halimiocistus wintonensis 'Merrist Wood Cream'

Halimiocistus wintonensis first occurred in the old West Hill Nursery of Messrs Hillier in about 1910. The nursery (only a garden centre now remains) was situated on a chalk slope which rises above and to the west of the city of Winchester. I first set eyes on this shrub in 1962 when I came to work at the Head Office which was situated in the nursery surrounded by a wealth of rare and unusual trees and shrubs. There was also a rock garden which had seen better days but which still supported an interesting collection of dwarf shrubs and slow-growing conifers. It is in this garden that the hybrid occurred, at least that's my guess for no one seems to remember.

It is believed to be the result of a hybrid between *Halimium ocymoides* and *Cistus salviifolius,* possibly 'Prostratus', both of which with others of their kind had long been grown and propagated by Hilliers at the West Hill Nursery or No.1 as it was referred to by the staff. It is a dwarf evergreen shrub of bushy habit up to 60cm (2ft) high and up to twice as much across. Both the shoots and small leaves are covered with a soft grey-white wool becoming dull

Grindelia chiloensis

- HARDY
- SUN
- MOST WELL-DRAINED SOILS
- EVERGREEN
- ZONES 9–10

× *Halimiocistus wintonensis* 'Merrist Wood Cream'

- HARDY IN MILD AREAS, BUT MAY NEED PROTECTION ELSEWHERE
- SUN
- WELL-DRAINED PREFERABLY LIME-FREE SOILS
- EVERGREEN
- ZONES 8–9

green and less densely hairy later. The flowers in late spring and early summer are like small single roses 5cm (2in) across, the five white petals having a crimson-maroon stain just above the yellow base. The flowers open in the morning and remain well into the afternoon before they are shed to be replaced the next day by a fresh crop. It received an Award of Merit from the Royal Horticultural Society in 1926.

In 1978 on a specimen of this plant growing at Merrist Wood Agricultural College near Guildford in Surrey, a sport was noticed by lecturer John Whitehead. Its flowers were cream coloured while retaining the dark centre. This has since been introduced to commerce under the name 'Merrist Wood Cream'. Given the Mediterranean origin of the parents, the hybrid and its cultivar, not surprisingly, demand a warm sunny situation preferably in a well-drained soil and are best considered for warmer areas. In my experience, plants grown in a rich soil tend to grow fast and lush and as a consequence fall easier prey to frost and wind. They are excellent in warm coastal gardens and are most suitable for the raised bed, terrace, rock garden and scree or for a narrow border at the foot of a sunny wall.

Like their parents, × *Halimium* are not very long lived, their fragile branches often breaking apart in a sudden wind and a ten-year-old plant is unusual. Severe winters can kill the top growth and one should wait until spring before deciding what to do. If damage is superficial then a light pruning is all that is necessary. If the damage is more serious then the plant is best removed. The best precaution against loss is to maintain a stock of young plants from cuttings taken in late summer and overwintered under glass.

Very different in effect is *Halimium* 'Susan', a dwarf shrub broader than it is high with small grey leaves and an abundance of small bright yellow dark-eyed flowers in early summer. Originally thought to be a bigeneric hybrid, this shrub is undoubtedly a hybrid between *Halimium lasianthum* and *Halimium ocymoides*. It was raised in 1956 by J.E. Sammons.

× *Halimiocistus wintonensis*
(**Family:** Cistaceae)
Pronunciation: ha-lim-ee-ō-*kis*-tus
Meaning: hybrid, from the names of the parents, *Halimium* × *Cistus*
Pronunciation: win-ton-*en*-sis
Meaning: of Winchester where it was raised by Hilliers.

Hydrangea paniculata 'Unique'

Hydrangea paniculata in the wild has one of the largest distributions of any hydrangea being found in Japan, Sakhalin, Taiwan and Korea as well as in eastern and south-east China. In cultivation it is known for its large conical heads (panicles) of white flowers which appear any time from midsummer onwards, their ornamental effect usually continuing into early autumn when the florets become pink or rose tinted. Several cultivars are represented in cultivation, all of which are easily grown reaching 3–5m (10–15ft) and of similar spread.

Pruning consists of removing the previous year's shoots to within two or three buds of the base in March. This has the effect of producing strong shoots with correspondingly large flower-heads.

Opposite: *Hydrangea paniculata* 'Unique'
- HARDY
- SUN OR HALF-SHADE
- MOST SOILS
- ZONES 4–8

Pruning should begin, by the way, early on in life, say within two to three years after planting, when the bush has formed a basic framework of hard wood. If space is no object there is no need to prune and although the resultant flower-heads will be smaller they more than make up for this in their numbers.

The flower-heads of wild *H. paniculata* comprise numerous tiny yellowish white fertile flowers with a sprinkling of larger white sterile ray florets. In the cultivar 'Floribunda' the ray florets are more numerous and up to 4cm (1 1/2in) across. This is an old selection dating back to 1867 at least which is at its best from mid summer through to early autumn. It received an Award of Merit from the Royal Horticultural Society in 1953.

One of the most attractive of this group is 'Kyushu' which was collected by that great gardener the late Captain Collingwood ('Cherry') Ingram as a seedling on sacred Aso-san, a volcano in Kyushu, Japan in 1926. It is extremely vigorous assuming small tree size eventually if unpruned and flowering in mid and late summer. The preponderance of fertile flowers give the large panicles an attractive fluffy appearance. 'Pink Diamond' is another with a mass of sterile ray florets raised by Robert and Jelena de Belder in their arboretum nursery at Kalmthout in Belgium. The large conical flower panicles turn pink then rose and finally crimson. It was given an Award of Merit by the Royal Horticultural Society in 1989.

By far the most popular and widely grown cultivar of *H. paniculata*, however, is 'Grandiflora' which was first introduced to Europe (Holland) by Philipp von Siebold from Japan in about 1860. Most, if not all, the flowers are sterile ray florets, large and conspicuous forming a densely packed conical head which is white to begin with turning, with age, purplish pink and then brown. It flowers from late summer into early autumn at which time it is spectacular, especially when regularly pruned, although the resultant obese heads are not to everyone's taste. In the same class as 'Grandiflora' is 'Unique', the white sterile florets turning a lovely pink with age. It received an Award of Merit from the Royal Horticultural Society in 1989.

All the cultivars enjoy a fertile soil whether acid or alkaline and benefit from a regular mulching with well-rotted manure, compost or leaf mould. A word of caution regarding pruning; regular pruning, even when it is accompanied by mulching or feeding, tends eventually to exhaust these shrubs They are, however, easily propagated from cuttings in summer.

Hydrangea paniculata
(**Family:** Hydrangeaceae)
Pronunciation: hi-*drang*-gee-a
Meaning: from the Greek *hydor* (water) and *aggos* (a jar) referring to the cup-shaped seed capsules
Pronunciation: pa-nik-ew-*lah*-ta
Meaning: with flowers in panicles.

Hydrangea serrata 'Preziosa'

Most people are familiar with the bold mop-headed hydrangeas which are commonly planted in gardens and parks up and down the country, especially in seaside resorts of the south and west. They are derived from a Japanese species called *Hydrangea macrophylla* and their large rounded heads of colourful but sterile florets place

them in a group known as the Hortensias. Less familiar is *Hydrangea serrata*, a smaller shrub to 1m (3ft) or slightly more, and as much across. It is also a native of Japan where it is found as a woodlander in the mountains of Honshu, Shikoku and Kyushu as well as the island of Cheju-do (Quelpaert) off the coast of South Korea.

H. serrata is said to have been introduced into European cultivation in 1843 and it is much better suited to small gardens than *H. macrophylla* which, when happy, can cover a fair piece of ground. Being a mountain species *H. serrata* is hardier than *H. macrophylla* differing also in its narrow, often lance-shaped, thinner textured leaves and more slender shoots. The flowers, borne in late summer, are carried in slightly dome-shaped or flattened heads (corymbs) at the ends of the shoots and are of lace-cap form, the central mass of tiny fertile bluish flowers ringed by conspicuous blue or pink sterile ray florets. These often change colour as they age.

H. serrata is mainly represented in British cultivation by several cultivars of which 'Bluebird' is perhaps the most well known. This is more vigorous than the wild type reaching 1.7m x 2m (5ft x 6ft) eventually, with pale blue or pink ray florets. It also flowers earlier in the season and is one of the hardiest cultivars being fairly tolerant of drought. It was given an Award of Merit by the Royal Horticultural Society in 1960. 'Grayswood' is another Award of Merit plant (1948) of similar size to the last, if not taller, but with white ray florets ageing to pink and, in a sunny situation, to bright red. 'Diadem' is much smaller, to 75cm (2½ft) compact in habit with lace-cap heads borne on side shoots all up the stems which start to open in June. It received an Award of Merit from the RHS in 1963 and was raised by the late Michael Haworth-Booth in his nursery near Haslemere in Surrey. The ray florets are a clear blue or pink. Quite different is 'Preziosa' in which the flower-heads are rounded and composed entirely of conspicuous sterile ray florets which are pale pink at first with darker margins, ageing to a clear crimson blotched and stained a deeper shade. This is a very popular hydrangea because of its

Hydrangea serrata
'Preziosa'

- HARDY
- SUN OR HALF-SHADE
- MOIST BUT WELL-DRAINED SOILS, FLOWER COLOUR DEPENDING ON ACID OR ALKALINE SOIL
- ZONES 6–8

Hydrangea serrata
(**Family:** Hydrangeaceae)
Pronunciation: hi-*drang*-gee-a
Meaning: from the Greek *hydor* (water) and *aggos* (a jar) referring to the cup-shaped seed capsules
Pronunciation: se-*rah*-ta
Meaning: saw toothed (the leaves).

hardiness and small size (1.3m (4ft)) with flower-heads resembling those of a Hortensia but smaller. It is a cultivar of German origin introduced by Messrs Kordes in 1963.

The type of soil can have an effect on flower colour; the ray florets of 'Bluebird' and 'Diadem' are more inclined to colour blue on acid soils, the more acid the soil the richer the blue. If these cultivars are grown on a neutral or only slightly acid soil their florets will be pink. 'Preziosa' develops its richest colour when grown on a neutral to slightly acid soil; the florets develop violet shades on strongly acid soils.

Soil reaction apart, *H. serrata* and its cultivars need a fertile soil (they are gross feeders) and enjoy an annual mulch of well-rotted manure, leaf mould or similar organic matter. They also require a ready water supply during times of drought despite the tolerance some cultivars have of these conditions. A position in sun or half-shade suits them and there should be no need for pruning except in the unlikely event of shoots being killed back in severe winter. If plants do become leggy or mis-shapen they will take pruning, even hard pruning, which is best carried out in spring. They can be propagated by cuttings in summer.

Itea ilicifolia

Augustine Henry (1857–1930) was an Irish physician who in 1880 left home for China to join the Imperial Chinese Maritime Customs Service. For seven years (1882–89) he was stationed at Ichang (now Yichang) on the Yangtze which is about 1,609km (1,000 miles) from the sea. Ichang, however, was an important treaty port as the head of steam navigation on this major river and situated as it was just below the entrance to the Yangtze Gorges, it was regarded as the gateway to the interior. Social life for a European in Ichang was fairly limited and predictable, and Henry began taking long hikes in the mountains as well as exploring the nearby gorges.

His interest in plants initially was mainly limited to those of medicinal value but, fascinated by the variety on all sides, he took to collecting specimens, sending them for identification to Kew Gardens. It was not long before his curiosity grew into a passionate interest fuelled by the encouragement of the Kew botanists and the knowledge that many of his finds were new to science. Although most of his collections were dried specimens he did make a number of seed and plant introductions, one of which was *Itea ilicifolia*, a cheerful evergreen which Henry found quite common in the hills above Ichang. Seeds sent to Lord Kesteven of Casewick flowered for the first time in 1895 and when E.H. Wilson sent further consignments in 1900 it became firmly established in cultivation. A dense bushy shrub of 3–4m (10–13ft) or more in cultivation, it is most often given the protection of a warm wall against which its leafy stems can be trained to cover a considerable area. There is a plant trained against wires on the west-facing wall of my house in

Itea ilicifolia
(**Family:** Escalloniaceae)
Pronunciation: ee-*tee*-a
Meaning: the Greek name for a willow
Pronunciation: ee-lik-i-*fo*-lee-a
Meaning: with leaves like *Ilex* (holly).

Hampshire which in nine years has reached 5m (16ft) in height and almost that in spread, the pliable young shoots extending 60cm (2ft) or more in some years.

It is worth growing for its dark glossy green leaves which have the appearance of a holly with their prickly teeth, but which are flatter and thinner in texture. During summer the flower-spikes appear from the shoot tips, lengthening and drooping until in late summer they are at their best – long pendulous tapering tassels of tiny greenish white flowers. Although attractive *en masse* the secret of these tassels is revealed in the evening when they impart to the air around a delightful honey-sweet fragrance which, like that of *Azara microphylla*, is usually detected in passing. The flowers remain open at night and many is the time I have stepped out, torch in hand, to see the insect visitors which include a goodly array of moths.

Itea ilicifolia is not hardy in the coldest inland areas where it is liable to shoot damage or defoliation in severe winters. It demands and deserves a warm sheltered site, not surprising considering its native home in those hot dry limestone hills above the Yangtze Gorges. It will grow in any well-drained fertile soil so long as extremes are avoided and is easily propagated from cuttings in late summer.

Below left: *Ilea ilicifolia*
- HARDY IN MILD AREAS, BUT MAY NEED PROTECTION ELSEWHERE
- SUN OR HALF-SHADE
- MOST WELL-DRAINED SOILS
- EVERGREEN
- ZONES 8–10

Ozothamnus ledifolius

The alpine zone on the summit of Tasmania's Mount Wellington above Hobart is a fascinating place for the plant enthusiast. It is situated about 1,270m (4,166ft) above sea level and consists of an undulating area of rough rocky terrain densely populated with low growing heath-like shrubs, mosses and grasses. Indeed, when I first set eyes on it one day in January 1988 I had to rub my eyes and

Below: *Ozothamnus ledifolius*
- HARDY
- SUN
- MOST SOILS
- EVERGREEN
- ZONES 9–10

look again for I could have sworn that I was standing on an Irish mountain in Kerry or Cork. The slanting wind driving a fine drizzle into my face, only reinforced the illusion. It was when I took a second closer look at the vegetation that I realised the emerald green pads and hummocks of moss were in fact flowering plants like Donatia and Abrotonella while the heath-like shrubs were members of the Australasian family of epacrids (*Epacridaceae*) which with few exceptions are notoriously difficult in British cultivation.

There were other shrubs too including *Ozothamnus ledifolius* which I first encountered almost 30 years ago when I joined Hilliers Nursery in Winchester. I regard this as one of the most underrated garden shrubs today and I am forever recommending it. It is a dense evergreen bush of compact rounded habit reaching 1m (3ft) by as much or more across. The downy stems are densely clothed with small narrow leathery leaves which are glossy dark green above and yellow beneath with the margins recurved. The whole plant is clammy to the touch and sweetly aromatic. The small dense heads of tiny white flowers are golden brown, reddish or a charming burnt sienna in bud crowding the tips of the branches in early summer. Both flowers, and the fluffy seed-heads which follow, give off a honey-like aroma especially noticeable in warm weather. As the flower-buds form some months before they open, their ornamental effect is considerable.

In British cultivation, *O. ledifolius* is the hardiest of its genus and seems tolerant of a wide range of situations ranging from dry well-drained or sandy soils to those of a cooler, damper persuasion. It prefers a situation in full sun and will survive all but the severest winters in most gardens. As a wild plant it is endemic to the mountains of Tasmania (found nowhere else) and was first introduced to British cultivation by Harold Comber from his expedition in 1929–30. Because of the aromatic secretion from the young shoots and leaves which is highly inflammable it is sometimes referred to in Tasmania as the 'kerosene bush'. I can vouch for its burning qualities having once disposed of an old plant which had been shattered during a gale. It will, I hasten to add, tolerate wind and is a good shrub for exposed gardens so long as it is not crowded with other more vigorous subjects. It contrasts well with cistus species and hybrids and other dome-shaped shrubs, such as hebes. It can be propagated from cuttings in late summer.

Ozothamnus ledifolius
(**Family:** Compositae)
Pronunciation: o-zō-*thăm*-nus
Meaning: from the Greek *ozo* (a smell) and *thamnos* (a shrub) referring to the leaves which are aromatic when bruised
Pronunciation: lay-di-*fo*-lee-us
Meaning: with leaves like *Ledum*.

Paeonia × lemoinei 'L'Esperance'

The tree peonies are regarded by their admirers as belonging to the aristocracy of garden plants along with the lily and the magnolia. Their history of cultivation which in China dates back to the Tang dynasty (AD618–907), probably earlier, is a rich and complex one to which numerous articles, books and learned treatises have been devoted. It all seems to have begun with the wild moutan *Paeonia*

suffruticosa, a now rare species from the mountains of Shaanxi (Shensi) and Gansu (Kansu) provinces in north-west China. This was originally valued and brought into cultivation by Buddhist monks because of its medicinal properties although no doubt its beauty of flower was not lost on them.

Over the centuries, it was increasingly cultivated for its ornamental qualities and the various hybrids and sports that arose were carefully propagated, nurtured and further distributed. By the end of the fifteenth century, moutans were known in many lovely forms, single and double, with white, pink and red – either alone or in combination – the main colours. Naturally, it was also grown by the emperors in their palace gardens and courtyards and its flower in art has come to represent the month of March and in design the season spring.

Moutans are said to have been introduced to Japan in the eighth century and in that country they were further bred and refined to produce the magnificent flowers we see today. The first live moutan to be seen in Britain was a plant introduced from China in 1787 by Sir Joseph Banks, Director of the Royal Botanic Gardens, Kew. This had a large double bloom, in colour purplish red at base fading to almost white at the petal tips. From then on for a hundred years moutans in variety continued to arrive by sea, usually aboard merchantmen of the East India Company.

One of the most important periods of peony introductions occurred around the middle of the nineteenth century when

Paeonia × lemoinei
'L'Esperance'

- HARDY
- SUN OR HALF-SHADE
- WELL-DRAINED, PREFERABLY NEUTRAL TO SLIGHTLY ACID, SOIL
- ZONES 5–8

Paeonia × lemoinei
(**Family:** Paeoniaceae)
Pronunciation: pie-*on*-ee-a
Meaning: from the Greek name *paionia*, meaning of Paion, physician to the gods
Pronunciation: la-*mwŭn*-ee-ee
Meaning: after Messrs. Lemoine of Nancy who first raised this hybrid.

Philipp von Siebold sent about 40 of the finest Japanese cultivars to Holland, and a few years later Robert Fortune sent to England many lovely cultivars from Chinese nurseries. Their flowers varied in colour, size and shape and caused great excitement among the horticultural fraternity. Sadly, few of Fortune's introductions survived for long due possibly to neglect, faulty cultivation or because they had been grafted onto weak or diseased stock.

Today, a wide range of moutan cultivars are imported into Britain each year and are available from specialist suppliers. Most are offered under Japanese cultivar names and vary in form from semi-double to anemone-form in a wide range of colours.

In the 1880s, two other tree peonies were discovered growing wild in west China and sent home to Paris by the missionary-cum-botanist Jean Marie Delavay. One of these, a shrub of 1–2m (3–6ft) with handsome deeply cut leaves and nodding or inclined deep purplish red, cup-shaped flowers 5–10cm (2–4in) across in June, was named after him – *Paeonia delavayi*. It is native to the Jade Dragon Mountains above Lijiang in north-west Yunnan and in 1986 I saw it growing quite commonly there on the lower slopes of the eastern flank beneath mixed conifer and broadleaf woodland. The other species discovered and introduced by Delavay was named *Paeonia lutea* in reference to its golden yellow flowers in late spring which have up to twice the normal number of petals – six to ten rather than five. Some forms have a red stain at the base of each petal and I have seen examples of these in the Cangshan Mountains above Dali in Yunnan, which is where Delavay and later George Forrest collected their plants.

P. lutea is a smaller growing shrub (sub-shrub rather) than *P. delavayi* its suckering stems normally reaching only 1m (3ft). There is, however, a splendid 'giant' version var. *ludlowii* collected by Ludlow and Sherriff in south-east Tibet near the Tsangpo Gorges in 1936. This differs most strikingly from the species in its more robust habit 2–2.5m (6–8ft) high and as much across, its larger, bolder leaves and its larger flowers, 10–12.5cm (4–5in) across, in late spring. Where space permits, this variety is worth growing for its foliage alone; it is quite spectacular. All three have been recognised by the Royal Horticultural Society – *P. delavayi*, Award of Merit in 1934; *P. lutea*, First Class Certificate in 1903 and *Paeonia lutea* var. *ludlowii*, Award of Merit in 1954.

There is in cultivation another group of tree peonies known as *P. × lemoinei* which are the result of crossing *P. lutea* with moutans (*P. suffruticosa*). The first seedlings were raised early this century by the famous French firm of Lemoine of Nancy and by Professor Louis Henry in the garden of the Paris Museum. A further range of hybrids was later raised by Professor A.P. Saunders in the USA using *P. delavayi*, *P. lutea* and *P. suffruticosa*.

Some of the most important of the early hybrids are still available, including 'Souvenir de Maxime Cornu' a Henry hybrid introduced in 1919 with very large heavy, fully double (rather too much so) flowers which are yellow, tinged with a mixture of brownish orange and red. They are strongly fragrant too. 'L'Esperance' is an exquisite Lemoine hybrid raised in 1909 with large semi-double yellow flowers, the petals arranged in two rows and stained red at the base. This is a tree peony of good constitution and was regarded by the late Michael Howarth-Booth – who had as fine a collection as any – as the finest tree peony for the garden ever raised. Other early hybrids include 'Alice Harding' (Lemoine 1936), with large fully double bright lemon yellow flowers and 'Chromatella' (Lemoine 1928), a sport from 'Souvenir de Maxime Cornu' with large heavy pure, sulphur-yellow flowers.

Among the Saunders hybrids 'Argosy' is perhaps the best known, in British cultivation certainly. It is a lovely peony with large single flowers up to 17cm (7in) across, the petals primrose yellow, carmine at base. It was awarded a First Class Certificate by the RHS in 1956.

All these hybrids flower from late spring into summer and are multi-stemmed shrubs to 2m (6ft) high. They will grow in most types of soil, including those over chalk, but thrive best in one which is well drained, neutral to slightly acid and fertile, while an occasional mulching with well-rotted manure is beneficial. They are quite hardy and suitable for most areas of Britain. However, as their young growths are liable to damage by spring frosts they should be given a sheltered site, or at least some form of temporary protection, should frosts be forecast. This does not apply, however, to *P. delavayi* or *P. lutea* and its variety which are less prone to damage.

The only serious disease to which tree peonies are susceptible is peony grey mould blight (*Botrytis paeoniae* and *B. cinerea*). These fungi affect the buds and shoots causing them to blacken and wither. Diseased material should be cut clean away and burned while spraying the young growths with Benlate, or similar, once at bud burst and then twice more at fortnightly intervals, will give some protection.

The species can be raised from seed, which should be sown when fresh, while the moutans and named cultivars of *P.* × *lemoinei* are normally increased by grafting on roots of *P. lactiflora* in winter. Grafted plants should be planted with the lower 7.5–15cm (3–6in) of the scion (grafted shoot) below soil surface. This is done to encourage the scion to form its own roots which makes for a stronger, longer lived plant. The large heavy-flowered cultivars may also need light staking or similar support to prevent them becoming damaged in heavy rain or wind.

Perovskia atriplicifolia 'Blue Spire'

Perovskia atriplicifolia
(**Family:** Labiatae)
Pronunciation: pe-*rof*-skee-a
Meaning: after V.A. Perovsky (1794–c1857), a Russian general
Pronunciation: ă-tri-pli-ki-*fo*-lee-a
Meaning: with leaves like *Atriplex*.

Perovskia atriplicifolia is native to the western Himalaya and Afghanistan where it grows in dry, desert conditions in valley bottoms and sometimes on stony slopes, as in the Chitral Valley of Pakistan and in Ladahk where it grows in vast quantities to the exclusion of other vegetation. It is said to have been introduced to British cultivation in 1904 but it is not commonly grown despite its hardiness, graceful habit and late flowering. In cultivation it is best treated as a sub-shrub, pruning the long stems hard back in early spring thus promoting strong erect new shoots which can reach 1.2m (4ft). These are four-angled and covered in a grey-white powder-like down while the pairs of coarsely toothed grey-green leaves to 5cm (2in) long are aromatic when bruised.

The small violet-blue two-lipped flowers are carried in terminal spikes during late summer and early autumn and are a lovely contrast against the pale stems. Even better than the type is 'Blue Spire' a selection of more upright habit to 1m (3ft) the leaves variously cut and lobed but never as finely as those of the related *P. abrotanoides*, of which it is sometimes regarded as a hybrid (*P.* × *hybrida*). 'Blue Spire' also differs from *P. atriplicifolia* in its larger spikes (panicles) and it is without doubt one of the loveliest and most useful late summer flowering garden shrubs.

It was introduced to Britain apparently from a German nursery as *P. atriplicifolia erecta* and was first distributed under its present name by Messrs Notcutt of Woodbridge, Suffolk who gained for it an Award of Merit from the Royal Horticultural Society in 1963. It enjoys best a sunny well-drained position and is quite happy in poor sandy or chalky soils. I have seen it combining most effectively with purple-flowered clematis of the Viticella group on the terraces at Knightshayes Court in Devon and Graham Thomas has described elsewhere its beautiful effect when planted with the pink-flowered Japanese anemones. It can be propagated by cuttings in summer.

Perovskia atriplicifolia 'Blue Spire'
- HARDY
- SUN
- MOST WELL-DRAINED SOILS
- ZONES 6–9

Pittosporum tenuifolium
'Tom Thumb'

- HARDY IN MILD AREAS, BUT MAY NEED PROTECTION ELSEWHERE
- SUN
- WELL-DRAINED LIME-FREE SOILS
- EVERGREEN
- ZONES 9–10

Pittosporum tenuifolium 'Tom Thumb'

In January 1985 I realised an ambition when I visited New Zealand and saw for the first time in the wild many familiar plants I had come to know in British gardens. One of them was *Pittosporum tenuifolium*, called Kohuhu by the Maoris. It is found in both islands being common in coastal and lower mountain forests and scrub-lands and is easily recognised by its almost black polished branches and branchlets densely crowded with wavy margined pale shining evergreen leaves. The small pendulous bell-shaped flowers are chocolate-purple in colour and almost hidden in the foliage. Their strong honey-like fragrance is especially noticeable in the evening.

P. tenuifolium is a large shrub or small tree variable in the wild and even more so in cultivation where it has produced a goodly number of cultivars some of which are suitable for the smallest gardens. One such is 'Tom Thumb' a slow growing shrub which in time makes a compact, dome-shaped or globular bush 1m (3ft) or more high and the same across with small leaves that emerge pale green and quickly turn a burnished dark purple. It makes an excellent subject for a rock garden, raised bed or for a narrow border at the foot of a wall. It also does well in a container on the terrace. I have yet to see it flowering but its merit lies in its small size and coloured foliage.

'Irene Paterson' which was found in the wild near Christchurch by Mr G. Paterson, is a taller growing shrub, the young leaves white

Pittosporum tenuifolium
(**Family:** Pittosporaceae)
Pronunciation: pi-*tos*-po-rum
Meaning: from the Greek *pitta* (pitch) and *sporum* (a seed) referring to the sticky seeds
Pronunciation: ten-ew-i-*fo*-lee-um
Meaning: with thin leaves.

becoming densely speckled green and grey-green. In 'Eila Keightley', the small rounded pale green leaves have a central splash of yellow and yellowish green with cream coloured midrib and veins, pink tinged in winter. This is a sport of 'Gloria Robinson' which arose in the Masterton nursery of Messrs D. Robinson in New Zealand. 'James Stirling' is another tall shrub with much smaller, pale green rounded leaves than normal. It was raised by James Stirling in New Zealand in 1966. There are also several golden and silver variegated forms which, however, eventually become trees though they can be clipped or pruned if desired. One of the hardiest and most ornamental variegated pittosporums is *P.* 'Garnettii', a dense, fast growing, compact, broadly columnar shrub or small tree up to 6m (20ft) or more with flattened leaves of pale green and grey, irregularly margined cream, and with pink or red spots. It was raised by Burton's Nursery of Christchurch, New Zealand. It is thought to be the hybrid and is named after Arthur Garnett who found it. All forms of *P. tenuifolium* are frost tender to some extent and are best planted in a sheltered situation. They thrive best in warmer and coastal areas. They can be propagated by cuttings in late summer while the typical green form can also be grown from seed which it often produces in some quantity.

Ptelea trifoliata 'Aurea'

If you look at the leaves of the hop tree *Ptelea trifoliata* through a hand-lens you will see that it is peppered with shining dots which are transparent when held against a light. These are tiny glands which, when the leaf is bruised, give off a strong aroma. They are a characteristic of this group of low-growing trees and shrubs, none of which is common in cultivation.

P. trifoliata itself is shrubby in habit but can develop in time into a small bushy-headed tree, trained to a single stem if necessary, and reaching eventually 5–6m (16–20ft) high and quite as broad. The leaves are clover shaped, with three shining green leaflets which often colour a rich yellow before falling in autumn. In early or mid summer the greenish white, tiny flowers are strongly scented of orange blossom and are borne in loose clusters up to 7.5cm (3in) across. They give way to drooping clusters of pale green, disc-like fruits 2.5cm (1in) across, the seed surrounded by a thin veiny wing. These fruits often hang on to the branches through winter. Both the bark and the young fruits possess the same strong aroma as the leaves and because of their bitterness the seeds were once used as a substitute for hops in brewing, hence the English name.

In the wild *P. trifoliata* is native to south-east Canada through eastern USA into Mexico. Its roots are aromatic but bitter and pungent to the taste and contain the alkaloid berberine. Early Americans imagined that anything tasting sufficiently bitter might be a substitute for quinine hence the name quinine tree in some

***Ptelea trifoliata* 'Aurea'**
(**Family:** Rutaceae)
Pronunciation: *tel*-ee-a
Meaning: Greek name for an elm, the winged fruits are similar
Pronunciation: tri-fo-lee-*ah*-ta
Meaning: with three leaves (leaflets)
Pronunciation: *ow*-ree-a
Meaning: gold (the leaves).

Ptelea trifoliata 'Aurea'
- HARDY
- SUN OR HALF-SHADE
- MOST SOILS
- ZONES 4–9

parts of the USA. The hop tree is quite hardy in cultivation and adaptable to most soils, except very dry and wet sites, preferring good drainage. It is happy in sun or shade and in the wild is often found as an understorey in moist woodlands. Its cheerful polished green foliage is even brighter in the cultivar 'Aurea' which was raised in Germany at the end of the last century. Here the leaves are rich yellow at first becoming a lime green by late summer. The colour is never harsh and because of this it fits easily into the garden landscape. It is one of the most acceptable yellow foliaged shrubs I know. *P. trifoliata* can be propagated by cuttings in summer and from seed when available and fertile. 'Aurea' is normally grafted by nurserymen on seedlings of the type.

Rhododendron occidentale

In June 1988 I found myself attending a Perennial Plant Study Weekend held in Seattle, Washington State. I had been asked to speak on perennials in the wild in China and as an added inducement, the organisers had promised to take me after the meeting on a trip to the Siskyou Mountains. It was an exciting prospect and I could hardly wait for the journey to begin. My guides for the trip were Denis Thompson, Sharon Coleman and Dan and Evie Douglas. I could not have asked for more friendly and amenable companions. Over a period of four days we made a round trip which took us south along the Oregon coast to the Siskyous on the Californian border then north to Seattle again. We saw a great number of exciting plants and had a lot of fun along the way but one of the most satisfying moments for me was seeing the Western azalea *Rhododendron occidentale* in the wild for the first time.

I shall never forget the circumstances for we had just visited Cape Blanco and were returning to the main highway when I suddenly spotted in a passing field a tree full of large birds. I yelled for Dan to stop and seconds later I was on the fence line training my binoculars on what proved to be a dozen Turkey vultures that now flapped away at our unwelcome attention. It was while I was standing there above the roadside ditch that I detected a delicious smell which drifted along the hedge from several azaleas in full flower. They were shrubs of 1–2m (5–6ft), some in full sun, others in shade, with loose terminal trusses of funnel-shaped white blooms flushed pink with a yellow stain on the inside of the upper lobe.

Seeing such a garden-worthy ornamental growing wild in a hedge took me by surprise but this was just the beginning and during the following two days we encountered it in many locations, especially in the Siskyous where it commonly grows in wet creeks and in moist places generally. Its fragrance is invariably the first clue as to its identity and whereabouts. The amount of pink or rose and yellow in their flowers varied from plant to plant and we saw some fine selections which would have graced any garden. It was interesting to find them flourishing often in the full glare of the sun (it was very hot at the time) with their roots in a moist soil.

Not surprisingly, *R. occidentale* and its hybrids enjoy similar conditions in cultivation and it is one of the best azaleas for stream and pond sides and in all but badly waterlogged situations. It is also one of the best hardy summer-flowering shrubs, for too long neglected by gardeners in favour of the more obvious merits of the Exbury and Knaphill azaleas. Its leaves are capable of rich colours in autumn.

Rhododendron occidentale
(**Family:** Ericaceae)
Pronunciation: ro-do-*den*-dron
Meaning: the Greek name for *Nerium oleander* from *rhodo* (red) and *dendron* (a tree)
Pronunciation: ok-ki-den-*tah*-lee usually pronounced ok-si-den-*tah*-lee
Meaning: western.

Rhododendron occidentale
- HARDY
- SUN OR HALF-SHADE
- MOIST LIME-FREE SOILS
- ZONES 5–8

The flowers, by the way, can be enjoyed over a long period in early and mid summer, emerging after the foliage has expanded. It is widely distributed in the wild in California and Oregon and was first introduced to British cultivation apparently by the Cornish collector William Lobb in about 1851, though it must have been seen earlier, however, by David Douglas and other European and American travellers. It is the only azalea native west of the Rockies and is regarded by some authorities as a western representative of the East American *Rhododendron arborescens*. The late flowering paler flowered *R. occidentale* has been crossed in the past with other American and some Asiatic azaleas to produce the so-called Occidentale hybrids which offer a range of pastel shades.

All are fragrant, late spring to early summer flowering bushes 1.7–2m (5–6ft) tall. Those most usually available include 'Delicatissum', soft yellow in bud opening cream with a slight pink tinge; 'Exquisitum', creamy white flushed pink with frilled margin and an orange flare (First Class Certificate after Trial at Wisley Gardens 1968); 'Graciosum', soft yellow at first becoming white tinged with pink at the margin and with a large orange flare (Award of Merit from the RHS in 1908); 'Irene Koster', white flushed crimson-pink, very fragrant; 'Mrs Anthony Waterer' creamy white with a pink tube and a yellow flare, very fragrant and with reliable leaf tints in autumn (First Class Certificate from the RHS in 1892) it is one of the oldest of A. Waterer's hybrids; and 'Superbum' buff pink in bud opening white, flushed pink with frilly margins and large orange flare (Koster 1901).

The *Occidentale* hybrids require an acid soil in sun or half-shade and prefer a moist situation, or at least one that does not dry out in summer. They can be propagated from seed or selected named forms from cuttings in early summer.

Romneya trichocalyx

The Matillija poppy, or Californian bush poppy as it is also known is variously regarded by botanists as being of a single or two species depending on which club they belong to. Members of the 'Lumpers Club' regard romneya as being of a single species *Romneya coulteri*, while members of the 'Splitters Club' take the opposite view and recognise the existence of a second species, *Romneya trichocalyx*; plants intermediate in character between the two being regarded as hybrids (*Romneya × hybrida*). Consideration of the facts leads me to regard *R. trichocalyx* as no more than a subspecies or variety of the other but in deference to established usage I shall treat them here as separate species.

Although included here as shrubs they are in truth sub-shrubs, their fleshy top-growth often dying down in winter especially in cold climates. Indeed, in many gardens they are treated as herbaceous and their stems, or what may remain of them, are cut clean away from the base each year in late winter. New growth appears from below ground in spring, quickly expanding to produce blue-green stems up to 2m (6ft) tall or more depending on growing conditions. The leaves are similarly coloured, the larger ones deeply divided. Towards the ends of the stems, around midsummer, slender branches are formed, most of them producing at their tip a single large beaked flower-bud. These open over an extended period from early summer to early autumn to reveal a large bloom of typical poppy shape, the five white petals crimpled like satin surrounding a corona of golden-orange stamens with a crimson base.

The flowers are flamboyant and delicately fragrant and, given their continuous appearance. This is one of the most reliable of all shrubs for summer display. According to Philip McMillan Browse, Director of Wisley Gardens, who is familiar with them in the wild, the fragrance is reminiscent of magnolias. Romneyas do, however, in my experience at any rate, seem to pick and choose for whom they will grow. I know of people who have tried for years to establish them without success while others I have met complain of them becoming weeds. They have a fleshy creeping and penetrating root-stock which in time will provide a thicket of leafy stems. Penetrating is the key word as I have heard of them pushing up shoots through paving and tarmac and once under a house wall into someone's library indoors.

In the garden they prefer a warm sunny situation and a rich but well-drained soil acid or alkaline. Badly drained soils are often the reason for premature deaths. A border or bed beneath a south- or south-west-facing wall particularly suits them but given their invasive nature they should not be planted in critical sites or near other less robust plants unless efforts are made to confine their spread.

Romneya coulteri was first discovered by the Irish physician and botanist, Thomas Coulter, in April 1832 growing in the hills around San Gabriel south of Los Angeles. Another 43 years passed before it was introduced into the British Isles. It was named by William Harvey in honour of Coulter and their mutual friend Dr Romney Robinson. Appropriately, its first flowering in cultivation took place at the Glasnevin Botanic Garden in Dublin in the autumn of 1876 when a single bud opened, a prelude to a magnificent display the following year. It was awarded a First Class Certificate by the Royal Horticultural Society in 1888. Whether regarded as a variety of *R. coulteri* or as a species in its own right, *R. trichocalyx* in cultivation certainly appears to be a more elegant, less robust plant with slender stems and thinner more deeply cut leaves. The flowers, too, are more clustered and the buds rounded rather than beaked and clothed with bristles. If anything it is even more invasive when established.

'White Cloud' is said to be a hybrid (or intermediate) between the above two. It was raised in the USA over 40 years ago and was first distributed by Louis Edmunds from his nursery in Danville, California. First offered in Britain by Hilliers Nurseries in 1971 'White Cloud' is noted for its robust bushier habit, more glaucous foliage as well as its larger flowers produced over a longer period. When I was Curator at the Hillier Arboretum in the 1970s we had

Romneya trichocalyx
(**Family:** Papaveraceae)
Pronunciation: rom-*nee*-a
Meaning: after the Rev. Dr Thomas Romney Robinson (1792–1882), Irish astronomer
Pronunciation: tri-kō-*kă*-liks
Meaning: with a hairy calyx.

Romneya trichocalyx
- HARDY
- SUN
- MOST WELL-DRAINED SOILS
- ZONES 8–10

a colony of 'White Cloud' thriving in the dry sandy soil of a large bed which over the years it came to dominate. It had been planted there some time in the 1960s.

In the wild, *R. coulteri* is native to a restricted area of California from the Santa Ana Mountains to San Diego County while *R. trichocalyx* occurs over a much wider area in Ventura and San Diego Counties and across the Mexican border into Baja California where it is found in Chaparral and coastal Sage Scrub.

Propagation is by seed which, however, is often unsatisfactory. Otherwise it is by rooted suckers or root cuttings in late winter.

Viburnum plicatum 'Pink Beauty'

Viburnum plicatum
'Pink Beauty'

- HARDY
- SUN OR HALF-SHADE
- MOST WELL-DRAINED SOILS
- ZONES 5–9

One of the many fine ornamental plants introduced to British cultivation from China by Robert Fortune is *Viburnum plicatum*. It had long been cultivated in Japanese and Chinese gardens when first described by the German physician and botanist Engelbert Kaempfer in 1712 yet not until Fortune's introduction in 1846 was it seen by British gardeners. It is, of course, now a familiar sight here with its snowball-like heads of white sterile flowers freely borne along the branches on a shrub capable eventually of reaching 3–4m (10–13ft) by as much across. Even better is *V. plicatum* 'Grandiflorum' with larger flower-heads becoming pink-tinted with age and a more tiered habit of growth.

Another viburnum long grown in Chinese and Japanese cultivation was named *Viburnum tomentosum*. This differed in its distinctly tiered branching and broad flattened crown as well as in its flattened (lace-cap) heads of tiny cream coloured, fertile flowers with several conspicuous large white sterile, marginal florets. This shrub was first introduced to Britain from Japan by Charles Maries for the Veitch Nurseries in about 1865 and later by E.H. Wilson. It was not until some years later that botanists realised that the snowball flowered *V. plicatum* was no more than a sterile garden form of the wild *V. tomentosum* and the two were placed under the same name, *V. plicatum* (this being the first name validly published) with the wild form referred to as *forma tomentosum*.

In British cultivation the latter is mainly represented by several named selections including 'Mariesii' (one of Maries introductions), 'Lanarth' and 'Rowallane', all of which have a wide-spreading, flat-topped habit and large white lace-cap heads that cream the tiered branches in late spring and early summer. 'Rowallane', which was introduced to commerce from the garden of that name in Northern Ireland but which originated at Rostrevor in the same province, is the least vigorous of the three, also the marginal florets are slightly pink tinted and it is more reliable than 'Mariesii' in producing its red turning to black fruits. It received an Award of Merit from the RHS in 1942 and a First Class Certificate 14 years later.

An Award of Merit in 1930 was also received by 'Lanarth' which is considered the most vigorous, while 'Mariesii' is probably the most well known though not necessarily the best of them. 'Lanarth' certainly will reach 3–4m (10–13ft) in time by as much, usually more, across. All three are generally much wider than high. More recent in appearance are 'Cascade', a seedling of 'Rowallane' with larger flower-heads and freer fruiting, raised by the Dutch nursery firm of J. Shoemaker, Boskoop and introduced to commerce in 1970, and 'Summer Snowflake' raised by R.F. Michaud of the Alpenglow Gardens in Surrey, British Columbia, Canada from Japanese wild collected seed and introduced to commerce through the UBC Botanic Garden Plant Introduction Scheme in 1985.

'Nanum Semperflorens' is a Japanese seedling of dense bushy habit found by a Mr Watanabe in the wild on Mt. Fuji and introduced to British cultivation by Mr K. Wada of the Yokohama Nurseries. It produces flowers throughout summer but is normally at its best early in the season. Although capable of reaching 2m (6ft) it can be kept fairly low by a careful pruning in summer. This also encourages it to delay flowering until summer and early autumn. In October 1990 I visited the Watanabe Nurseries at Gotemba south of Tokyo, where I was shown several 3m (10ft) specimens of 'Nanum Semperflorens' that had been propagated from the original. Highly thought of by North American viburnum fans is 'Shasta' introduced to commerce in 1979 by the US National Arboretum. It reaches 2m (6ft) or so by twice as much across and is very free flowering. 'Pink Beauty', meanwhile, is a fairly upright selection taller than broad with smaller leaves and smaller flower-heads, the marginal florets becoming pink tinted with age creating a charming effect. It is said to have been raised in the United States.

All the above are hardy and of easy cultivation in most soils, acid or alkaline, preferring one fertile and moist but well drained in sun or half-shade. They are superb accent plants among otherwise low planting and make ideal specimens on banks, especially above water or in lawns or woodland beds where their tabulated manner of growth can best be appreciated. For this reason they are very effective in association with buildings, breaking up too harsh vertical lines. No pruning is necessary so long as plenty of elbow-room is allowed to accommodate their spread. If it is desired to restrict their height this is easily achieved by pruning out the leading shoots as they appear. This also helps encourage a more pronounced table-top effect. In some cultivars the leaves change to a dark red or purplish bronze in autumn before falling. They can be propagated by cuttings in summer.

Viburnum plicatum
(**Family:** Caprifoliaceae)
Pronunciation: vee-*bur*-num
Meaning: the Latin name for *V. lantana*
Pronunciation: pli-*kah*-tum
Meaning: pleated (the young leaves).

AUTUMN

To most people autumn is the death knell of summer, the closing of the year when deciduous trees and shrubs lose their leaves and herbaceous plants wither away. A sad time for some perhaps, but not for the gardener who discovers in autumn the year's most brilliant effects of dying foliage and ripening fruits. A host of shrubs, many of which have already contributed flower, fragrance or ornamental leaves to the pleasure of other seasons, reserve for autumn their finest display. But whilst autumn is for many shrubs an excuse for a final fling it is for a select few a time of flowering and the well-stocked and intelligently planted garden will have both elements represented.

Acer circinatum 'Monroe'

Compared with eastern North America there are few maples native to the western states and provinces of this vast continent, only three in fact and one of these a rarely seen (in cultivation) maple of the Rocky Mountains. The other two, however, are widespread especially *Acer circinatum*, the vine maple, so called apparently because in its native habitat when growing beneath large dark canopied conifers it will become a tall, viny-stemmed, slender tree in its efforts to reach the light. According to D.C. Peattie in *A Natural History of Western Trees* (out of print), its name refers to its 'intermittent habit of sprawling on the ground like a running lasso for sometimes 6–9m (20 or 30ft)'. He goes on to say that the early French *coureurs du bois* (runners in the woods or trappers) in western Canada called it, for this reason, *bois du diable* (tree of the devil), from its devilish habit of tripping-up canoe-men as they plodded, heavily laden, weary and half-unseeing where they stepped, along the portage trails. Its slender branches, too, according to the plant explorer David Douglas were once employed by Indians in the North-west in making the scoop nets with which they took salmon at rapids and narrows in the rivers.

In an open situation the vine maple makes a large multi-stemmed shrub of rounded habit eventually 6–9m (20–30ft) high and as much through. Anyone who has travelled the highways of the Pacific North-west from British Columbia south to California in autumn will have seen the yellow or red leaves of this maple in roadside woods and creeks where it is commonly associated with Douglas fir, western red cedar and other conifers. Botanically, it belongs to the same group as the Japanese maples and is the only non-asiatic member of this group. This provides further proof in the eyes of plant geographers of the former existence of a land bridge between north-west America and eastern Asia across which plants and animals migrated.

The leaves are similar to those of *Acer japonicum*, rounded in outline with seven to nine pointed lobes of varying size. The drooping clusters of small red or purplish red flowers emerge with the leaves in spring and are quite pretty when seen close to. Unlike the Japanese maples, *A. circinatum* has not produced a host of seedling variations suitable for cultivation which makes the few that do exist all the more interesting. The most unusual, and also the most ornamental, is called 'Monroe' after Dr Warner Monroe a professor of philosophy from Portland, Oregon who found this plant as a seedling in 1960 in the coniferous woodland on the headwaters of the McKenzie River in the Cascade Mountains. Layers from this seedling established it in cultivation though it still is not common in British gardens.

A. circinatum 'Monroe' differs most remarkably from the typical plant in its leaves, which are divided to the base into between five and seven lobes and the lobes themselves are deeply cut and lobed in the manner of the better known *A. japonicum* 'Aconitifolium'. In

Acer circinatum
(**Family:** Aceraceae)
Pronunciation: ă-ker, usually pronounced *ay*-ser
Meaning: classical Latin name for maple
Pronunciation: ker-kin-*ah*-tum, usually pronounced ser-sin-*ah*-tum
Meaning: rounded, referring to the leaves.

Previous pages: *Acer palmatum* **'Osakazuki'** is one of the best Japanese maples for autumn colour.

my garden the leaves of 'Monroe' begin to change colour in late summer becoming flushed with red or purplish red, the colour intensifying before leaf fall. It is a most attractive maple of a strong upright habit at first, spreading later and probably reaching 4–5m (12–16ft) eventually. It is easy in cultivation like the vine maple itself and is particularly valuable to the gardener for its tolerance of drought and shade although, of course, the better the conditions the more luxuriant its growth. It is remarkable how well it does in dry soils and I remember its relatively firm, fresh appearance in the droughts of 1986 and 1989 when the Japanese maples were definitely flagging.

The vine maple is easily raised from seed so long as it has not been allowed to dehydrate, while 'Monroe' is propagated by grafting. In my experience, *A. circinatum* is relatively pest and disease free and given space and good growing conditions can more than hold its own with its more celebrated relatives from Japan.

Above left: *Acer circinatum* 'Monroe'
- HARDY
- SUN OR HALF-SHADE
- PREFERABLY LIME-FREE SOILS
- ZONES 6–8

Above: *Amelanchier lamarckii*
- HARDY
- SUN OR HALF-SHADE
- PREFERABLY LIME-FREE SOILS
- ZONES 5–9

Amelanchier lamarckii

Amelanchier lamarckii is the shrub most often sold in the British nursery trade as *Amelanchier canadensis*, a name which correctly belongs to quite a different shrub. Having said that, its origin remains a puzzle. According to experts, it is almost certainly from eastern North America where, however, it is apparently unknown in a wild state. To see it at its best in the wild one need go no further than south-east England where, between Kent and Dorset it is not uncommon in the open woodland of oak, birch or pine, on sandy acid soils, even flourishing where the ground is peaty and waterlogged in winter. It is also found in similar situations in parts of Holland and north-west Germany.

How *A. lamarckii* first arrived in these places is a source of great argument but it was already known in Surrey in 1893 and there is substance in the suggestion that it may have arrived in Europe some time in the early nineteenth, if not late eighteenth century. Most probably it was first cultivated in a garden, later establishing itself in the wild via bird-sown seed. Whatever doubts exist as to its pedigree there can be none concerning its ornamental merit. Apart from a preference for acid soils it appears to have everything going for it as a garden shrub. Hardy, vigorous, adaptable to dry or damp sites, it is equally happy in half-shade as in full sun, although it does flower and fruit better in an open situation whilst its autumn colour is better there.

It is a large multi-stemmed shrub up to 6–8m (20–25ft) high on average, though it is capable of more, and as much across. It is easily encouraged to form a single main stem by judicious pruning and many specimens naturally become tree-like if left alone. While pruning of the longer current year's shoots in summer can limit its size and, incidentally, encourage greater freedom of flowering, it is perhaps not suitable to the really small garden even though its all-round qualities are tempting. On this score there are few shrubs its equal. I have included it here for its exceptional autumn colour, the neatly toothed leaves turning to yellow, orange and red. It could just as easily be included for its spring effect when the slender branches in mid and late spring erupt with loose clusters of snow-white flowers and, at the same time, the coppery, grey downy young leaves emerge. It also produces small red fruits ripening to purplish black around midsummer hence the popular name Juneberry for these shrubs in America. In Britain the name Snowy mespilus is most commonly applied to *A. lamarckii* and its relatives. The fruits, although sweet and edible, are not normally borne in sufficient abundance in Britain and those that are, are frequently taken before ripening by blackbirds and others.

In borders and beds *A. lamarckii* has a dominant effect in spring and autumn but it is as an isolated specimen, especially in a lawn, that this shrub really comes into its own. It is easily propagated by seed (which comes true) as well as by cuttings in summer or alternatively by layering.

Amelanchier lamarckii
(**Family:** Rosaceae)
Pronunciation: ă-me-*lan*-kee-er
Meaning: from the French name 'amelancier' for *A. ovalis*
Pronunciation: la-*mar*-kee-ee
Meaning: after the French naturalist Chevalier Jean Baptiste de Monet Lamarck (1744–1829).

Aronia arbutifolia

The red chokeberry is one of three species native to eastern North America where it is widespread especially in woodlands and bogs. It was among the first American plants to be introduced to Britain where it was already in cultivation in 1700.

It is a multi-stemmed shrub of vigorous erect habit suckering to form, in time, dense clumps or thickets up to 3m (10ft) tall. Clusters of small white flowers in late spring are followed by bright red fruits which although at their best in autumn sometimes continue into early winter. They are not readily eaten by birds because of their astringent taste hence the common name chokeberry. The principal reason for growing this shrub, however, is the autumn colour. The finely toothed leaves up to 8cm ($3^1/2$in) long are dark green above and grey downy beneath during summer changing in autumn to red, crimson or reddish purple. It is a shrub of easy culture, hardy and adaptable to most soils and situations though fruiting best in full sun. Given its suckering capacity and height it is probably best planted at the back of a border or in a semi-wild area or woodland margin of the garden.

It is a variable species and there are several named selections of which 'Erecta' is commonly available. This is more strictly erect in habit than the type though similar in other respects. Propagation is by seed, cuttings in summer or simply by division of the clump using a fork and secateurs or a sharp spade.

Aronia arbutifolia
(**Family:** Rosaceae)
Pronunciation: a-*rŏ*-nee-a
Meaning: from aria the Greek name for *Sorbus aria*
Pronunciation: ar-but-i-*fo*-lee-a
Meaning: with leaves like *Arbutus*, the Strawberry tree.

Aronia arbutifolia

- HARDY
- SUN OR HALF-SHADE
- MOST SOILS
- ZONES 5–9

Berberis sieboldii

Berberis sieboldii
(**Family:** Berberidaceae)
Pronunciation: *ber*–be-ris
Meaning: from the Arabic name
Pronunciation: see-*bōld*-ee-ee
Meaning: after Philipp Franz von Siebold (1796–1866), German doctor who introduced and named many Japanese plants.

Philipp von Siebold was a remarkable man by anyone's standards. Born in Bavaria, he worked a short time for the Dutch East India Company in Batavia and then, in 1923, was chosen to accompany a special Dutch embassy to Japan. Whilst there he practised medicine including cataract operations (he had graduated as an eye specialist) which gave him tremendous prestige with the Japanese and allowed him to travel extensively where no other foreigners had been allowed. From his travels he made large collections of ethnological objects as well as zoological and botanical specimens including seeds and live plants. He also collected maps, most of which he secured from friendships with the Court Astronomer in Tokyo and others well placed. This proved his undoing, for in 1828, he was accused of being a spy and was imprisoned for a year. He returned to Holland in 1830 fortunate to have escaped execution and equally fortunate to have shipped his collections home before imprisonment.

Von Siebold established a nursery in Leiden where he propagated and sold many of the plants he had introduced from Japan. They included a number of species which are still popular in gardens such as *Hydrangea paniculata*, *Malus floribunda* and *Spirea thunbergii*. Several of his introductions were named after him including *Berberis sieboldii* a choice, dwarf deciduous shrub which, curiously, remains uncommon in cultivation. Rarely more than 1m (3ft) in height it spreads by suckers to form rounded clumps or patches of reddish slender, spiny stems. The spines are also small and slender and the plant is, as a result, more easily handled than most of its kin.

The leaves of *Berberis sieboldii* are relatively large, 2.5–8cm (1–3in) long and margined with short fine bristles. Dark glossy green above they turn to rich orange then red before falling in autumn. The clusters of small yellow flowers in spring, meanwhile, are replaced by glossy red fruits. As a dwarf shrub for autumn colour *Berberis sieboldii* is hard to beat. It is quite hardy and suitable for most soils but performs best in a dry sunny situation especially in sandy soils. This is surprising since, in the wild, it is commonly found growing in bogs in company with *Ilex crenata*. Propagation is by cuttings in summer or by seed when available.

Callicarpa bodinieri 'Profusion'

Callicarpa bodinieri
(**Family:** Verbenaceae)
Pronunciation: kă-lee-*kar*-pa
Meaning: from the Greek *kallos* (beautiful) and *karpos* (a fruit)
Pronunciation: bo-din-ee-*e*-ree
Meaning: after Emile Marie Bodinier (1842–1901), French missionary and plant collector in China.

Anyone seeing the berries of this shrub for the first time can be excused for thinking they are not real. So far removed are they in colour from the usual that most people have to stop and examine them in detail. They vary from lilac to purple, are 3–4mm (1/8in) in diameter and are produced in dense axillary clusters all along the shoots in autumn. The lilac flowers in mid summer are tiny and relatively insignificant, from a distance at least.

The species *Callicarpa bodinieri* is an erect shrub 2–3m (6–10ft) tall with narrow downy slender-pointed leaves that turn madder purple or reddish purple in a good autumn. In the wild it occurs in the Chinese provinces of Sichuan, Hubei and Shaanxi. It is most often represented in cultivation by variety *giraldii* which differs but little.

Although the callicarpas have normal (perfect) flowers they appear to berry better and more reliably when several seedlings are planted in close proximity to effect cross-pollination. This is fine if you have a large garden or arboretum but not if your garden is of the pocket handkerchief variety. Fortunately, there is a cultivar of *C. bodinieri* var. *giraldii* named 'Profusion' which, apart from being free berrying is reliably so when planted as an individual. Even young plants berry well and their colour is a striking violet. The shrub occurred as a seedling in the nursery of T. van Veen and Sons of Boskoop, Holland and was introduced to commerce in 1962.

Like others of its clan, 'Profusion' is amenable to most soils although it thrives best in one with plenty of humus. It is quite hardy and should be planted preferably in full sun to encourage ripening of the shoots as well as for flower and berry production. As its main merit is its autumn berries and foliage, it is perhaps best grown in a border with other shrubs that will provide ornament at other seasons. Propagation is by cuttings in summer whilst *C. bodinieri* and var. *giraldii* may be grown from seed.

Below left: *Berberis sieboldii*
- HARDY
- SUN
- PREFERABLY LIME-FREE SOILS
- ZONES 6–8

Below: *Callicarpa bodinieri* 'Profusion'
- HARDY
- SUN
- MOST SOILS
- ZONES 6–8

Calluna vulgaris 'Annemarie'

Considering the great number of cultivars of the heather or ling in cultivation, it comes as a surprise to many gardeners to learn that there is but a single species involved. Unlike the heaths (*Erica*), of which there are hundreds of species, *Calluna vulgaris* is the one and only and so unique is it that it has never been known to cross with any other members of its family though imagined hybrids between *Calluna* and *Erica* (× *Ericalluna*) have from time to time been offered by nurserymen.

One of the glories of late summer and early autumn occurs when moorlands, mountainsides and heaths are transformed from summer green and brown to a rich purplish pink haze as the heather blooms. Not long ago, I took a visiting Chinese botanist to the New Forest in Hampshire when the heather was at its peak. It gave me immense pleasure to see the look on his face when we stepped out of my car and beheld a sea of purple. The effect was accentuated by dark clumps of Scots pine and gold splashes of gorse (*Ulex minor*), stretching as far as the eye could see. A year previously, I had accompanied him in the mountains of his native Yunnan and there seen vast tapestries of alpine rhododendrons. His reaction on seeing the heather was akin to mine in Yunnan – a stunned silence.

Neither heather nor gorse is found in China (not even in gardens) and my friend's experience therefore, was doubly exciting. Other than the British Isles, heather is found wild over most of Europe, part of south-west Asia and in North Africa (north-west Morocco). A dwarf often carpeting evergreen, the heather, like most other members of its family, abhors lime in the soil, otherwise it has no particular fads and given full sun and an acid soil that does not dry out completely in summer, it will flourish and flower its heart out year after year.

The tiny flowers (both calyx and corolla are coloured) are densely borne on often long spikes and are rich in nectar, a fact which apiarists have long exploited. In some areas of Scotland and the north of England bee hives are still taken to the heather when in flower, the honey produced being highly prized. Over the years the wild heather populations have produced other prizes in the shape of sports and aberrations which the keen-eyed gardener has taken home and propagated. Hundreds of cultivars have come into cultivation this way and their names are legion. They vary in habit (bushy to prostrate) but rarely more than 50–60cm (20–24in) in height when flowering; foliage (green, grey, orange or gold); flower form (single or double); flower colour (purple, pink, red or white); and in various other ways.

According to personal taste, heather gardens can be colourful and exciting or predictable and boring. For a small garden certainly, they offer an easy and rapid means of achieving results added to which they are relatively trouble-free, their close dense growth smothering weeds and presenting a reasonable appearance throughout the year. However, being fast growing they benefit from an annual pruning

Calluna vulgaris
(**Family:** Ericaceae)
Pronunciation: ka-*loo*-na
Meaning: from the Latin *kalluno* (to cleanse); it was once used to make brooms
Pronunciation: vul-*gah*-ris
Meaning: common.

Calluna vulgaris
'Annemarie'
- HARDY
- SUN
- LIME–FREE SOILS
- EVERGREEN
- ZONES 5–7

of the old flowering shoots either immediately after flowering or when the new growth commences in spring. Old plants tend to become leggy or untidy and are best replaced – around every eight to ten years or so.

Although I would not have in my garden a bed or border devoted entirely to heathers nor even a mixture of heathers and heaths, I do have a small island bed in which grow several heathers and heaths together with a selection of dwarf conifers and shrubs. The two heathers I have chosen are 'Kinlochruel' and 'Annemarie'. The first of these is a dense compact cultivar with green foliage and spikes up to 25cm (10in) long of double white flowers which are at their best in late summer and early autumn. In the opinion of some heather buffs, it is easily the best double white heather and this seems to have been confirmed by the Royal Horticultural Society who in 1980 gave it an Award of Merit followed two years later by a First Class Certificate. It was found by Brigadier E.J. Montgomery as a sport on the cultivar 'County Wicklow' in his garden at Kinlochruel near Colintraive in Argyll, Scotland, in 1969.

Just as impressive is 'Annemarie'. Raised by Kurt Kramer of Süddorf, West Germany, as a sport on the cultivar 'Peter Sparkes' and introduced to commerce in 1980. It has a compact bushy habit and dark green foliage above which rise in early and mid autumn in 25cm (10in) spikes densely crowded with double, light pink flowers that gradually darken in colour to carmine-rose.

Similar in every way except that the flowers are a deep purple red is 'Red Star' another Kramer special. It occurred as a sport on 'Annemarie' and was introduced to commerce in 1984. It also flowers in early and mid autumn and is stunning when planted with 'Annemarie' and 'Kinlochruel'. An excellent single red heather by the way is 'Allegro', a sport of 'Alportii Praecox' introduced into commerce by P. Bakhuyzen and Sons of Boskoop, Holland in 1977. It has green foliage and 50cm (20in) spikes of deep red flowers in late summer and early autumn. Introduced in 1989, again by Kramer, 'Annabel' is another lovely heather, similar in habit and colour to 'Annemarie' but flowering two weeks earlier. Heathers are easily propagated by cuttings in summer.

Cornus florida 'Rainbow'

Cornus florida 'Rainbow'
- HARDY
- SUN OR HALF-SHADE
- MOIST BUT WELL-DRAINED LIME-FREE SOILS
- ZONES 6–9

In its native eastern United States the Flowering dogwood is a common sight in woodlands and thickets often along roadsides where its white flowers, before the leaves in mid or late spring, announce the arrival of spring. The 'flowers' are in effect large coloured bracts (modified leaves), four in number which surround the small crowded head of insignificant greenish true flowers. It is these showy bracts which give rise to the name Flowering dogwood for although all dogwoods flower only a small number have this striking characteristic. It was introduced to British cultivation in the early part of the eighteenth century and has been grown there ever since although it is not best suited to wetter areas. This is because it enjoys a continental climate where regular warm summers ripen growth and encourage free flowering.

In Britain it flowers best in south-eastern and eastern England and although old specimens can be found in gardens elsewhere flowering does not compare with that seen in drier areas. Indeed, I shall never forget during my years at the Hillier Arboretum in Hampshire the many American horticulturists visiting in spring who would cast an indifferent eye over *Cornus florida* which we grew in good numbers. 'Call that a dogwood?' was ever the unspoken comment. Although ours could not compete with those I have seen in Pennsylvania and Virginia they certainly earned their keep and with the bonus of autumn colour are well worth considering for the medium-sized to large garden.

It is for the autumn colour that I have included *C. florida* here and whilst the typical plant and its many white, pink or red flowered selections turn to glorious shades of red, purple and crimson the effect is even more impressive in those cultivars with variegated leaves. Currently, there are two of these available in general cultivation of which 'Rainbow' is the most frequently seen. It was first offered by the nursery firm of Frank Schmidt & Son of Boring, Oregon in 1969 although it had been found originally by Armond Marzelli of Canton, Ohio as a sport on a sprouting stump of the ordinary kind. The leaves are irregularly margined and splashed with yellow through summer becoming red suffused in autumn. At their peak they are a fiery two-tone red above and grey or pink tinted beneath, contrasting effectively with the green and yellow of the younger late colouring leaves. The flowers have white bracts.

Just as attractive is 'Welchii', a selection made by an American nurseryman Mark Welch about 1920 and first distributed by the Cole Nurseries of Painsville, Ohio in 1930. Here the leaves in summer are a combination of green, creamy white and pink, the pink intensifying through rose-red to red-purple in autumn. In the United States, a third variegated cultivar 'Cherokee Sunset' is considered by many who have seen it to be the best yet. This has the bonus of bright red new growth in spring and ample white bracted flowers. It arose as a sport on 'Cherokee Chief' and was introduced to commerce by H.A. Nicholson, Commercial Nurseries Co. of Decherd, Tennessee. Hopefully, it will reach British shores in the near future. Compared with the green-leaved cultivars these variegated kinds are slower growing. Two of the most satisfactory green-leaved cultivars for flower in Britain are 'Cherokee Princess' (white) and 'Cherokee Chief' (red).

C. florida and its cultivars enjoy best a moist but well-drained acid soil with plenty of organic matter. Although welcoming the partial shade of trees in hot, dry summers, in cooler climates it needs the benefit of full sun especially if free flowering is to be encouraged. Wet soils and shade or exposure to cold winds are an anathema to it. Propagation is by seed or, in the case of the named selections, by cuttings in early summer or by grafting. In North America *C. florida* is subject to a number of pests and diseases the most serious being a wilt disease, but this has not been reported in Britain.

Cornus florida
(**Family:** Cornaceae)
Pronunciation: *kor*–nus
Meaning: the Latin name for the European *C. mas*
Pronunciation: *flō*-ri-da
Meaning: flowering, the flowering dogwood.

Cotinus 'Grace'
- HARDY
- SUN
- MOST SOILS
- ZONES 5–8

Cotinus 'Grace'

At one time included in the genus *Rhus* as *Rhus cotinus*, the Venetian sumach *Cotinus coggygria* differs most strikingly from *Rhus* species in its entire rounded or egg-shaped leaves as well as in its fluffy smoky pink flower-heads which turn grey later, hence the alternative name of Smoke tree.

It is a common shrub in cultivation especially in one or other of its reddish purple or purple-leaved selections such as 'Notcutt's Purple' or 'Royal Purple'. In both, the colouration extends to the young shoots and to a lesser extent the flower-heads, providing a striking contrast to grey and green-leaved subjects. In the wild, *C. coggygria* is widely distributed from Central and Southern Europe eastwards to the Himalaya and China where it is generally found in dry valleys and on sunny hillsides in mixed scrub. I first saw it wild above the Greek theatre at Dodoni in Greece and much later, and more spectacularly, in the hills above the Great Wall in North China. Here it has been planted by the Chinese in huge quantities and its foliage in autumn paints the landscape red for miles around.

Cotinus
(**Family:** Anacardiaceae)
Pronunciation: *ko*-ti-nus
Meaning: from *kotinos*, Greek name for the olive (*Olea europaea*).

In the south-eastern states of Tennessee, Alabama and Texas in North America, grows the only other member of this genus – the American Smoke tree or Chittamwood, *Cotinus obovatus*. As a young man I was familiar with a large plant of this species growing in a park near Manchester. It was easily distinguished from nearby *C. coggygria* by its larger leaves (up to 15cm (6in)) long and its larger flower-heads. Since then I have seen this species flourishing on the dry alkaline soil of the University Botanic Gardens, Cambridge and on the chalk of Hilliers' West Hill Nursery, in Winchester, Hampshire where it reached 7m (22ft). There is an equally fine specimen in the Hillier Arboretum growing on acid sandy soil.

Although surprisingly uncommon in British cultivation – it was first introduced in 1882 – *C. obovatus* is a superb large shrub or small tree where space is available. The young leaves in spring are a lovely pinky bronze becoming a darker blue-green, offering in autumn various shades of red, purple and orange. Even in winter it provides interest in its grey to greyish brown bark which is divided into small plates rather like the scales of a fish. In both species of *Cotinus* the tiny insignificant male and female flowers are borne on separate plants. It is the hairs on the thread-like flower stalks that collectively make the flower-heads conspicuous and those of the male plant being larger are the more ornamental.

It was in 1977 that Peter Dummer, Master Propagator at Hilliers, first had the notion of crossing the two smoke trees. The following year using a containerised plant of 'Velvet Cloak' a rich dark purple leaved American selection of *C. coggygria* as the mother plant, he transferred pollen from *C. obovatus* growing in the Hillier Arboretum and by early autumn fruits had set. Seeds sown the following spring produced six seedlings all showing leaves intermediate in size and shape between the parents and extremely vigorous. In 1983 these seedlings had become well established in containers and one of them produced a massive flower-head, deep pink in colour some 30cm (12in) high by 28cm (11in) wide. The leaves of this plant were 10–15cm (4–6in) long, a light wine red when young darkening to plum red with age and colouring richly in autumn. Peter Dummer named this seedling 'Grace' after his wife and in November 1983 he submitted it to the Royal Horticultural Society, who gave it an Award of Merit. It also earned for Peter the coveted Reginald Cory Memorial Cup which is awarded annually to the raiser of what is judged to be the best deliberate hybrid shown to the Society during the year. In 1990 it received the society's ultimate accolade – a First Class Certificate.

Cotinus 'Grace' is proving to be a first-rate shrub or small tree for the garden. Like its parents it is hardy and adaptable to most soils acid or alkaline although wet or badly drained soils should be avoided. It performs best, however, in a well-drained none too rich soil and an open sunny situation. It is fairly tolerant of exposure as well as drought and like *C. obovatus*, it will probably reach 8m (25ft) high in time and in an ideal situation. Propagation is by cuttings in summer while the species may also be increased from seed when available. There need be no pruning except to reduce specimens considered too large or when training specimens to a single main stem. Care must be taken when pruning to keep the orange yellow sap from contact with the skin as it can cause a nasty rash or worse if it is inadvertently transferred to eyes or mouth. A yellow or orange dye is obtainable from the sap of both species and the scarcity of the American Smoke tree in the wild, is apparently, in part the result of its extensive felling for this purpose during the Civil War.

All the cotinus mix well with most other shrubs in bed or border but are best as isolated specimens in the lawn where their rounded habit can develop to the full.

Eriobotrya japonica

Almost every day in late autumn 1989 I received telephone calls or letters from people anxious to tell me about the flowering of a shrub whose sweet hawthorn fragrance filled their garden or courtyard. In each case I guessed the shrub to *Eriobotrya japonica*, the loquat, a plant which enjoys nothing better than a warm sheltered corner and plenty of sun to ripen its growths and initiate flower-buds. No one will forget that long dry English summer of 1989 and its benefits, as woody plants, or most of them, flowered and fruited as never before. The drought created problems too but no one who looked on the flowering of the loquat and savoured its delicious aroma begrudged the heat for this particular triumph.

It is, alas, in Britain certainly, no more than an occasional pleasure and not one to be expected every year. In southern Europe where summer temperatures are consistently high the loquat flourishes, flowers and fruits to everyone's satisfaction and the piles of small yellow to orange, pear-shaped fruits on sale in stores and street markets are ample testimony to this. The skin of the fruit is thin and delicate while the flesh is orange and juicy, tasting of a mixture of apple and apricot. Being cultivated in countries as far apart as Italy, Israel, California and Brazil the fruits are available throughout the year. They can be eaten fresh, used in fruit salads or made into jam or compote. The four to nine large shiny seeds should be removed prior to eating or preparation. These are commonly brought home by curious gardeners from holidays in the sun and if sown without delay can result in a handsome pot plant for the home.

It is as a foliage plant that the loquat is most admired and even if it never flowered it would be worth growing outside in the sheltered garden or courtyard for its leaves alone. An evergreen shrub or small tree, the loquat is in the same league, foliage-wise, as some of the woodland rhododendrons such as *Rhododendron macabeanum* and the evergreen magnolias *Magnolia grandiflora* and *Magnolia delavayi*. The loquat's leaves, from 15–30cm (6–12in), differ from all these, however, in their toothed margins while the boldly veined, deep glossy green upper surface grey downy when young contrasts well with the greyish brown downy undersurface.

Eriobotrya japonica
(**Family:** Rosaceae)
Pronunciation: e-ree-ō-*bot*-ree-a
Meaning: from Greek *erion* (woolly) and *botrys* (a bunch of grapes), referring to the woolly flower head.
Pronunciation: ja-*pon*-i-ka
Meaning: of Japan.

Although named as from Japan where it has long been extensively cultivated, the true native distribution of the loquat is considered by some authorities to be central China. The plant hunter E.H. Wilson found it was fairly common in the area of the Yangtze Gorges, enjoying no doubt the warm ledges above the river and its tributaries. In 1988 I too saw it there on high cliffs in the lower reaches of the last gorge just above Yichang. It is, however, as in Japan, most frequently found in the gardens and courtyards of temples and monasteries where it is sometimes represented by impressive specimens. It was first introduced to British cultivation in 1787 by Sir Joseph Banks then Director of the Royal Botanic Gardens Kew.

In British cultivation the loquat is mostly found in milder areas and even there it is best given the protection of a warm wall or woodland. It is sometimes found growing quite well in town or city gardens elsewhere and may even form fruit occasionally but these rarely ripen. When happy it can reach as much as 9m (30ft) in height in time but specimens half this height and width are more normal. The flowers which are formed in summer have creamy white petals and numerous stamens and are borne in crowded heads, the individual flowers opening over several weeks in late autumn.

It enjoys best a moist but well-drained soil preferably on a neutral to slightly alkaline soil though it will tolerate others so long as extremes are avoided. In countries enjoying regular hot summers it will tolerate a fair amount of shade but otherwise is best given plenty of light. In some countries it is occasionally affected by fire blight but this is not a problem in Britain. Propagation is by seed when available or by cuttings in late summer.

In countries where the loquat is cultivated for its fruits there are several named selections available. There is also a handsome form 'Variegata' in which the leaves are streaked and margined white. Unfortunately, it is rarely ever available in the nursery trade.

Eriobotrya japonica

- HARDY IN MILD AREAS, BUT MAY NEED PROTECTION ELSEWHERE
- SUN OR HALF-SHADE
- MOST MOIST BUT WELL-DRAINED SOILS
- EVERGREEN
- ZONES 8–11

Above: *Euonymus alatus*

- HARDY
- SUN
- MOST SOILS
- ZONES 5–9

Euonymus europaeus
'Red Cascade'

- HARDY
- SUN
- MOST SOILS
- ZONES 4–7

Euonymus alatus

This is probably the most distinct and easily recognised of the spindleberries as well as being one of the most impressive and reliable of all shrubs for autumn colour. It is a densely branched shrub of rather spreading habit attaining in time 2–3m (6–10ft) and as much, if not more, across. It is, however, relatively slow growing and is quite suitable initially for small gardens where it is best planted as a specimen in a lawn or bed. In larger gardens I have seen it planted in groups of between three and five plants providing a spectacular show in autumn when the leaves turn a characteristic rich rose-scarlet. The four-angled young branches gradually develop corky outgrowths – wings or flanges – which give them a curious prehistoric appearance, especially in winter when leafless. Indeed, some plants look more like a piece of modern sculpture. The fruits are purplish red in colour, deeply two- to four-lobed and containing as many scarlet coated seeds. When produced in abundance they are quite attractive often remaining on the branches after leaf fall.

In the wild *Euonymus alatus* is found in north-east China, Korea and Japan where it grows in thickets and woods. I have seen it growing in hillside scrub below the Great Wall north of Beijing where it rubbed shoulders with deutzias, philadelphus and spiraeas. It was first introduced to western cultivation in 1860 and is now an accepted member of any shrub collection worth its salt. It is bone hardy and easy on most soils, acid or alkaline, preferring an open especially sunny situation to produce its best autumn display. It is propagated by cuttings in summer.

'Compactus' is an American selection which grows slowly to 2m (6ft) high or more and as much across. Its shoots often lack wings while its autumn colour is every bit as good as that of the type.

Euonymus alatus
(**Family:** Celastraceae)
Pronunciation: ew-*on*-i-mus
Meaning: the Latin name for *E. europaeus*
Pronunciation: ah-*lah*-tus
Meaning: winged, referring to the shoots.

Euonymus europaeus 'Red Cascade'

To anyone living in chalk or limestone country the common spindleberry is a familiar shrub of hedgerows, scrub and woodland margins and clearings. It is found on other soils, too, but nowhere is it as abundant as on alkaline soils. It ranges throughout Europe except the far north and the Mediterranean coast. It is a large shrub up to 4m (13ft), in some circumstances making a small bushy tree as much as 7m (25ft) high, the green shoots contrasting with the reddish purple shoots of *Cornus sanguineus* with which it often grows. The tough white wood of the spindleberry or spindle tree was once used to make spindles, skewers and pegs as well as being fashioned into viola bows, keys for the virginal and toothpicks.

The opposite leaves turn purple or reddish purple in autumn when at the same time, the loose pendulous clusters of colourful fruits drape the branches. Each fruit consists of a four-lobed red capsule that splits open to reveal the orange coated seeds. These fruits are poisonous and can prove fatal if eaten in quantity, although their taste is hardly what you would call appetising. The flowers which precede them in mid or late spring are small and yellowish green and are of no ornamental merit.

The spindleberry is variable in its fruiting qualities and several selections have been named over the years of which 'Red Cascade' is by far the most ornamental. Raised by Messrs Jackman of Woking, Surrey before 1949 it is reliable and free fruiting, the richly coloured fruits densely crowding the arching branches which become almost pendulous under their weight. Commonly seen as a dense mound 2m (6ft) high or more, it makes a superb feature in autumn but has little else to offer ornamentally. It received an Award of Merit from the Royal Horticultural Society in 1949.

Scale insects are sometimes a problem on spindleberries while *E. europaeus* is a host to blackfly especially at flowering time. Propagation is by cuttings in summer or by seed.

Euonymus europaeus
(**Family:** Celastraceae)
Pronunciation: ew-*on*-i-mus
Meaning: the Latin name for *E. europaeus*
Pronunciation: oy-rō-*pie*-us
Meaning: of Europe.

Fothergilla major

If you can tear yourself away from the spectacular autumn tints of Japanese maples at Westonbirt in Gloucestershire you will soon discover that there are other shrubs contributing to the magical effect of Britain's oldest and most visited arboretum. There are spindleberries (*Euonymus*) and viburnums which stop you in your tracks and berberis that sparkle like bonfires. None of these, however, can hold a candle to *Fothergilla major* whose rounded leaves are transformed when summer ends into yellow and old gold, painted and clouded with orange and red. At their peak they offer as rich a fusion of colours as you are likely to see anywhere and are capable of brightening even the dullest day.

Native of the Allegheny Mountains from Virginia to South Carolina in the USA, it was first introduced to British cultivation sometime before 1780 but was subsequently lost until re-introduced to Kew from the Arnold Arboretum, Massachusetts in 1902. Curious that so fine a shrub should have been neglected. Its popularity this century, however, has ensured its spread and survival in cultivation and it is not uncommon in gardens large and small and is ever present in any arboretum worthy of the name. It is relatively slow in growth with multiple rather erect main stems gradually increasing in size to 2–3m (6–10ft) eventually. Taller than wide, it makes a splendid specimen in a lawn or border and given the space, is even more impressive when planted as a group of three or five. The neat thimble-shaped clusters of flowers are borne on the leafless twigs in mid or late spring and an established bush at this time looks most effective.

The individual flowers are quite small and without petals, their collective effect being due to their numerous white stamens with yellow anthers, while as a bonus they possess a delicious honey-like

Fothergilla major
- HARDY, BUT NEEDS SHELTER FROM COLD WINDS
- SUN OR HALF-SHADE
- MOIST BUT WELL-DRAINED LIME-FREE SOILS
- ZONES 5–8

aroma. The casual observer viewing these flower-heads would not connect them with those of the witch hazel (*Hamamelis*) to which family it belongs.

Like the witch hazels, *F. major* does not care for limy or chalky soils and does best in a moist acid but free-draining loam that does not dry out in summer. For the best leaf effects it should be planted in a position open to the sun but sheltered from cold winds. Given its relatively compact habit it should require no pruning. Propagation is best accomplished by cuttings taken in summer since seed, when available, is not so easily germinated by the amateur.

Seed grown plants are variable both in habit and in leaf and you could plant in your garden six seedlings or more, each of which would exhibit its own characteristics. In my experience, however, few if any prove disappointing and *F. major* has to be one of the élite of autumn colouring shrubs. In addition, it is rarely troubled by either pest or disease. No wonder it has received an Award of Merit from the Royal Horticultural Society in 1927 and a First Class Certificate in 1969.

Fothergilla major
(**Family:** Hamamelidaceae)
Pronunciation: fo-tha-*gil*-a,
Meaning: named after Dr John Fothergill (1712–80), English physician who grew North American plants
Pronunciation: *mah*-yor
Meaning: larger (than *F. gardenii*).

Mahonia × media 'Lionel Fortescue'

Anyone who has ever seen *Mahonia lomariifolia* will have experienced the overwhelming desire to possess this evergreen aristocrat, for such it is with its upright stems and fabulous foliage. The largest specimen I have seen grows in that fine collection planted by the Smith-Barrys at Fota in Cork Harbour.

M. lomariifolia was first introduced from western Yunnan by Major Lawrence Johnston, creator of Hidcote Manor Gardens, at Chipping Campden in Gloucestershire, in 1931, while accompanying the Scottish plant hunter George Forrest. The small fragrant yellow flowers are crowded into erect cylindrical spikes in bold clusters at the ends of the shoots and together with the stiffly spreading deeply divided leaves present a magnificent spectacle in autumn. Unfortunately, it is suitable only for the mildest areas and warm sheltered positions elsewhere. It was in order to circumvent this disadvantage that several people in the 1950s and 1960s considered crossing *M. lomariifolia* with the well known and hardier *Mahonia japonica* which, as a point of interest, is a native of China (probably a form of *M. bealei*) long cultivated in Japan from whence it was first introduced (hence the name).

The first successful hybrids between these two mahonias, however, occurred by chance in the Slieve Donard Nursery, Newcastle, Co. Down, in Northern Ireland. Seed gathered from a stock plant of *M. lomariifolia* had been sown some time in the late 1940s. Unknown to Donard's, some, at least, of the flowers on the mother plant had been fertilised with pollen from a nearby *M. japonica* and as a result a percentage of the seedlings proved to be hybrids. A mixture of seedlings were acquired by Messrs L.R. Russell of Windlesham,

Mahonia × *media* 'Lionel Fortescue'

- HARDY, BUT NEEDS SHELTER FROM COLD WINDS
- SUN OR HALF-SHADE
- MOST SOILS
- EVERGREEN
- ZONES 8–9

Surrey who in turn sold six to the late Sir Eric Savill, maker of the Savill Garden in Windsor Great Park. Sir Eric, having realised their significance, planted them in the garden, later naming one of them 'Charity' and two others 'Hope' and 'Faith'. Donard's in the meantime, named one of their remaining hybrid seedlings 'Winter Sun'.

All these mahonias are large shrubs eventually, with bold evergreen leaves composed of leathery spine-toothed leaflets, dark shining green above, paler below, arranged in pairs along a stiff stalk (rachis). The leaves are characteristically crowded towards the ends of the stems and branches forming handsome ruffs above which the bunches of yellow flower spikes emerge. Six other seedlings have been named from this hybrid – 'Rebecca', 'Roundwood' and 'Sarah' are first generation seedlings from 'Charity' raised at the Savill Garden. Of the remaining three, two are the result of a deliberate cross and one a self-sown seedling.

Mahonia × *media* 'Underway' appeared as a chance seedling in the garden of that name owned by the late Norman Hadden at Porlock in Somerset. Both parents were present. 'Underway' appears to be bushier than the others and perhaps more suitable for the small garden. In addition, its flowers are quite fragrant. Its leaves, however, lack the elegance of 'Lionel Fortescue' and this characteristic shows the influence of the *japonica* parent. 'Buckland' and 'Lionel Fortescue' on the other hand were raised in the late 1950s by the last named at his home The Garden House, in Buckland Monachorum, Devon. Michael Hickson, head gardener at Knightshayes Court in

Devon who was employed by Lionel Fortescue in the 1950s told me how he was entrusted with the job of transferring pollen from *M. japonica* to *M. lomariifolia* in a greenhouse there. From the resultant seedlings 'Buckland' was named by Lionel Fortescue while the seedling named after him is one he gave to the Savill Garden.

M. × *media* 'Lionel Fortescue' is an outstanding shrub, handsome in foliage and flower. The flowers are a rich yellow borne in dense, often branching spikes up to 40cm (16in) long. These are fairly erect in habit initially, spreading later. Flowering normally begins in late autumn (sometimes slightly earlier) and continues into mid winter or later, the flowers opening in succession upwards from the bottom of the spike. They possess a pleasant fragrance, faint to my nose but distinct and immediate to others. It is a hardy shrub given shelter from cold winds and is extremely vigorous, capable of reaching 3m (10ft) or more and as much across in under ten years. It can be pruned quite hard if necessary, preferably in summer and may need to be in order to prevent or correct a tendency, common to all these hybrids, to become 'leggy'.

Amenable to most soils, acid or alkaline, 'Lionel Fortescue' is a gross feeder and thrives in a humus rich loam that does not dry out in summer. Sun or half-shade and a position where its all round merit can conveniently be admired is recommended. If it can be seen all year through from a window all the better, but beware planting it too close to a path or entrance where its spiny leaves can be a problem. In 1975 the calibre of this mahonia was recognised by the Royal Horticultural Society with an Award of Merit while its raiser received the Reginald Cory Memorial Cup for the best deliberate hybrid shown to the Society that year.

Propagation of all the named cultivars of *M.* × *media* is by cuttings or leaf cuttings (with stem attached) in late summer.

Mahonia* × *media
(**Family:** Berberidaceae)
Pronunciation: ma-*hon*-ee-a
Meaning: after Bernard McMahon (died 1816), Irish born American horticulturist
Pronunciation: *me*-dee-a
Meaning: intermediate (between the parents).

Osmanthus heterophyllus 'Variegatus'

Osmanthus heterophyllus is one of those amusing plants which horticultural lecturers and botany teachers love to use to test the knowledge or awareness of their students. The dark green leaves of a young plant certainly are margined with prickles and, to the untutored eye, are not unlike those of a holly. But whereas holly leaves are borne alternately on the shoots those of the osmanthus are in pairs – a point which would not have escaped Sherlock Holmes had he been put to the test!

The holly-like nature of the evergreen leaves accounts for two other names by which this shrub has been known in the past, *Osmanthus aquifolium* and *Osmanthus ilicifolius*. The present name refers to the variable nature of the leaves which may be spiny or smooth depending on the size and age of the bush. As on a holly, the spines tend to disappear from leaves in the upper part of the bush with maturity. It is a large shrub of bushy habit capable of

Osmanthus heterophyllus
- HARDY
- SUN OR HALF-SHADE
- MOST SOILS
- EVERGREEN
- ZONES 7–9

reaching 3–5m (10–15ft) and as much across, even higher in warm situations especially in woodland shelter. The flowers which open in mid and late autumn are small and white, borne in clusters in the leaf axils and possess for their size a remarkably strong fragrance which fills the air around. It is a native of Japan and Taiwan where it is sometimes seen as a tree up to 10m (30ft) tall. It was introduced to Britain in 1856 by Thomas Lobb, a Cornishman whose brother, William, also a plant collector, travelled in South America and was responsible for introducing the Monkey puzzle (*Araucaria araucana*) as well as many other exotics.

O. heterophyllus, in its typical form, is sometimes planted as an informal hedge or screen but it is not suitable for the small garden. In such situations the slower growing and less rumbustious 'Variegata' is preferable. It is possible that there are in cultivation two different plants under this name but the one most usually available, which I recommend, is a shrub of dense compact habit, conical at least when young slowly maturing to 3m (10ft) or more. Its leaves are small and of variable shape, few spined or spineless and in colour green or greyish green with an irregular creamy white margin. It makes a perfect lawn specimen and would also look well in a large container on the patio or in the courtyard, though I have yet to see it used thus.

Attractive and cheerful throughout the year it becomes even more so in autumn when the twigs are crowded with sweetly fragrant flowers. Both the type and 'Variegata' are hardy in all but the coldest areas. Nevertheless, in severe winters 'Variegata', is subject to scorching, but the shoots will break anew when winter is past. Propagation is by cuttings in late summer.

***Osmanthus heterophyllus* 'Variegatus'**
(**Family:** Oleaceae)
Pronunciation: os-*mănth*-us
Meaning: from the Greek *osme* (fragrance) and *anthos* (a flower) referring to the fragrant flowers
Pronunciation: he-te-rō-*fil*-lus
Meaning: with variable leaves
Pronunciation: va-ree-a-gah-tus
Meaning: variegated.

Pyracantha 'Orange Glow'

Pyracantha 'Orange Glow'
- HARDY
- SUN OR HALF-SHADE
- MOST SOILS
- EVERGREEN
- ZONES 6–9

No autumn would be complete without the mass effects of the firethorns – *Pyracantha* species and hybrids. Whether they are grown as free-standing specimens in a bed or lawn or trained against a wall or fence, they are guaranteed to bring colour into the garden and are excellent value for money. Grown without support, they are best suited to gardens of medium to large size where they can be given ample space in which to develop. On a wall or fence they need to be kept under close control, training the stems and main branches to wires or similar support and likewise pruning or tying-in any shoots that attempt to grow outwards. Trained in this fashion, it is not uncommon to see old firethorns covering walls to 6m (20ft) high or more and the same across.

In the wild they are commonly found in thickets and scrub on hillsides and in ravines where they enjoy free drainage and full sun. *Pyracantha coccinea* is native to southern Europe and western Asia and its berry-clad branches in late summer and autumn are a familiar sight, for instance, in the sun-drenched hills of Italy especially in Tuscany where it shares many a stony place with hawthorn and Cornelian cherry (*Cornus mas*). Just as common in similar terrain is *Pyracantha crenatoserrata*, a native of China where it is widely distributed in Yunnan, Sichuan and Hubei, north to Gansu and Shaanxi provinces.

Both the above species are in cultivation though they are easily outnumbered by their hybrids of which 'Orange Glow' is still one of the best for general cultivation. Raised by Dr O. Banga at the University of Wageningen, Holland in 1930 and introduced to commerce in 1949, it is the result of a cross between *P. crenatoserrata* and probably *P. coccinea*. It is a vigorous evergreen with strong thorny branches well clothed with glossy-topped dark green leaves. The flowers in late spring and early summer cream the branches and a large specimen at this time is spectacular. This display, however, pales in comparison with the autumn performance, when from early autumn onwards the large crowded bunches of rounded berries slowly ripen through orange to a shining orange-red. Highly acclaimed in Holland where it is said to be resistant to the disfiguring scab disease, this splendid firethorn has few rivals.

Also considered scab resistant are 'Orange Charmer' and 'Golden Charmer', with orange and yellow berries respectively. Both originated in the nursery of Heinrich Bruns at Westerstede, Germany in 1950 and are said to be the result of crosses between *P. coccinea* and the Chinese *Pyracantha rogersiana*. Apart from scab, the main problem pyracanthas are likely to face is fire blight which, however, will not deter those determined to enjoy their many qualities. Hardy, except for some leaf scorch in the severest winters, they are amenable to most soils and situations preferring, however, a sunny position. Propagation of the named hybrids is by cuttings in late summer while seeds will produce seedlings of variable merit.

Pyracantha
(**Family:** Rosaceae)
Pronunciation: pi-ra-*kănth*-a
Meaning: from the Greek *pyr* (fire) and *akantha* (a thorn) referring to the spiny shoots and red berries.

Rhus glabra 'Laciniata'

There can be few gardeners who do not know the velvety-twigged stag's horn sumach *Rhus typhina* and its handsome cut-leaved selection 'Dissecta'. In winter, gaunt branches, their extremities covered in a dense pelt of reddish hair, identify this small tree or large shrub from all others, while the handsome pinnate leaves of summer lend to the garden a faintly subtropical air which explodes in autumn in fiery tints of orange, red and purple. Male and female flowers are borne on separate plants, the tiny greenish flowers of the female

Rhus glabra 'Laciniata'
- HARDY
- SUN
- MOST SOILS
- ZONES 3–9

carried in erect dense-packed downy conical heads which terminate the shoots of the year. These give way to tiny rounded fruits clothed with reddish bristles which remain intact until well into winter.

In the wild, *R. typhina* is native to eastern North America where it is widespread, especially on roadsides, railway embankments and in neglected areas of cultivation. Of wider distribution in North America is *Rhus glabra,* the smooth sumach which differs from the former in the absence of hairs from stems and leaves and in the bluish white bloom covering the shoots of the current year. It is also less inclined to form a tree though it possesses the same wide-spreading habit and the same tendency towards suckering. Indeed, even in cultivation it is not uncommon to find both sumachs, when neglected, occupying extensive areas with their strong suckering stems. I have especially in mind a colony of *R. typhina* near Winchester in Hampshire which covers a sizeable area of railway embankment having escaped from under the fence of a neighbouring property. Over the years the brilliance of its autumn foliage has persuaded more than one train driver to reduce speed for his passengers' benefit.

Of the two, *R. glabra* is the less commonly seen in cultivation although its autumn display is equal to that of the other. Even more desirable in this department, however, is *R. glabra* 'Laciniata' in which the leaflets are deeply lobed creating an exotic fern-like effect which is hard to beat. Both *R. glabra* 'Laciniata' and *R. typhina* 'Dissecta' by the way are female forms, which means the crimson fruit clusters continue the show through winter.

Both these sumachs and their fern-leaved selections are among the toughest and most adaptable of all woody plants, being suitable for most soils and situations although, considering their suckering tendencies, I would not recommend them for planting in a fine lawn. Left alone, *R. glabra* will reach 2–3m (6–10ft), occasionally more in cultivation, with a similar spread, while *R. typhina* is capable of at least twice this. Suckering, of course, if tolerated, considerably increases the spread. The size of the bush can be controlled by an annual pruning in early spring. Stems cut to the ground or low down will sprout strong new shoots with even finer foliage. Pruning in this instance is best done with long-handled loppers taking care not to get the sap on your hands or face. Their pithy stems when cut exude a yellowish white sap which can cause an irritating rash.

Propagation is most conveniently accomplished by suckers removed in winter. Both *R. typhina* and *R. glabra* were first introduced to cultivation in Britain early in the seventeenth century while *R. glabra* 'Laciniata' was discovered in the wild near Philadelphia by one Elias Durand in the mid 1800s. The commonly cultivated fern-leaved form of *R. typhina,* by the way, is correctly 'Dissecta' although it is most often grown and catalogued as 'Laciniata'.

Of pests and diseases there are none of any significance although *R. typhina* certainly and *R. glabra* probably are sometimes affected by Verticillium wilt which, however, is rarely fatal. The leaves and young shoots of both sumachs are rich in tannin and when dried can be used to dye wool or cotton tan to dark brown.

***Rhus glabra* 'Laciniata'**
(**Family:** Anacardiaceae)
Pronunciation: rus
Meaning: the Latin name for the European species *Rhus coriaria*
Pronunciation: *glăb*-ra
Meaning: smooth, without hairs
Pronunciation: la-kin-ee-*ah*-ta
Meaning: slashed or cut into narrow divisions, referring to the leaflets.

Sorbus poteriifolia

At the south-west end of Jermyns House in the Hillier Arboretum, Hampshire is a small private garden hidden from public view by hedges and borders. During the 1960s and 70s this was the late Sir Harold Hillier's secret place where he planted, often for the first time in Britain, some of his rarest and most desirable dwarf shrubs and plants. He had ready access to this garden through the French windows of his small study and it was a favoured visitor indeed who was shown the contents of this Aladdin's Cave. One special 'treasure' here was *Sorbus poteriifolia*, the world's smallest mountain ash, which Sir Harold had planted in a raised bed where it grew in a well drained gritty soil exposed to the sky. It never failed to elicit excited comment especially in autumn when the leaves turned to a rich red and the red fruits turned white.

Not far away from this gem grew another dwarf mountain ash *Sorbus reducta* but this species although attractive enough has none of the other's elfin charm. In cultivation the stems of *S. poteriifolia* are rarely more than 10cm (4in) tall, creeping at the base and rooting to form low colonies. The pinnate leaves are small, neat and glossy green above while the clusters of pink-tinted flowers in summer give way to tiny green fruits which change colour and swell.

Hardy enough in cultivation, it prefers a moist but well-drained cool soil that does not dry out in summer and is ideally suited to the peat garden or to a raised bed or rock garden where one can keep a close eye on its development and where it can more easily

Sorbus poteriifolia

- HARDY
- SUN
- MOIST BUT WELL-DRAINED PREFERABLY LIME-FREE SOILS
- ZONES 5–7

be protected from stronger neighbours.

For many years, Hilliers grew this species under the name *Sorbus pygmaea* (Pygmy Sorbus) which seemed most appropriate and it was with great reluctance that the name was changed to the present one. This was to conform with the International Code of Botanical Nomenclature which states that a name to be valid must, among other requirements, be published together with a description. Unfortunately, *S. pygmaea* was not and even if it had, the earlier name *S. poteriifolia* would still have taken precedence on grounds of priority.

In the wild *S. poteriifolia* is native to a few localities in the mountains of north-west Yunnan and northern Burma above 3,000m (10,000ft) altitude. It was first successfully introduced into western cultivation by the plant hunter Frank Kingdon-Ward from the Seingkhu Valley of north-east Burma in 1926 and from neighbouring valleys on at least two subsequent occasions. It remained scarce, however, in gardens and if it had not been for Sir Harold Hillier this choice species might well have been lost to cultivation. It can be propagated from cuttings in summer or by carefully detaching rooted stems. It can also be grown from seed if these are gathered before the birds get them and given a period of cold treatment in the fridge before sowing.

Sorbus poteriifolia
(**Family:** Rosaceae)
Pronunciation: *sor*–bus
Meaning: Latin name for the Service tree *S. domestica*
Pronunciation: po-te-ree-i-*fo*-lee-a
Meaning: with leaves like *Poterium.*

Viburnum furcatum

I first saw this viburnum in the old No. 4 Nursery of Hilliers at Chandlers Ford near Southampton back in 1963. Today, *Viburnum furcatum* is available from specialist nurseries and can be found in connoisseurs' gardens.

In the wild it is mainly native to Japan where it grows in thickets and forest clearings in the mountains. It is also found in the Kuriles, Sakhalin and Taiwan as well as the Korean islands of Cheju-do (Quelpaert) and Dagelet. It is a large shrub up to 3m (10ft), often taller in the wild, with nut brown stems noticeably erect at first, spreading more later in life. The branches form tiers which add considerably to the ornamental effect while the paired leaves are heart-shaped 10–15cm (4–6in) long and boldly veined.

It has two seasons of special effects, one of which is in late spring when the foliage is emerging and the flattened heads of small white flowers are borne. Each head is ringed with conspicuous white sterile flowers similar to those of the Guelder rose *Viburnum opulus*. These give way in autumn to heads of red ripening to purplish black berries; the leaves turn to either a rich claret red or purple.

E.H. Wilson, who knew more about shrubs than most, considered *V. furcatum* difficult in cultivation, like its eastern American counterpart *Viburnum lantanoides*, the Hobble bush. I disagree, however. Both enjoy a sheltered, especially woodland situation with no competition from tree roots and a soil which retains moisture in summer. Other than that they seem hardy enough and unfussy

Viburnum furcatum

- HARDY, BUT PREFERS SHELTERED POSITION
- SUN OR HALF-SHADE
- MOST SOILS, PREFERABLY LIME-FREE
- ZONES 6–8

as to soil type, growing equally well in those of acid and alkaline reaction. Some authorities claim that it must have shade and in countries enjoying regular hot summers this is probably true but a specimen in the Hillier Arboretum in Hampshire thrives in an open sunny situation in a sandy loam, its leaves colouring in autumn.

Although first introduced to Western cultivation in 1892 it has never been common in gardens. The same, however, could equally be said of a number of other fine viburnums. For their combination of pleasing habit, bold foliage, elegant flowers and rich autumn tints these shrubs have few rivals. They are propagated by seed when available or by cuttings taken in summer.

Viburnum furcatum
(**Family:** Caprifoliaceae)
Pronunciation: vee-*bur*-num
Meaning: Latin name for the European *V. lantana*
Pronunciation: fur-*kah*-tum
Meaning: forked, referring to the leaf venation.

Viburnum opulus 'Xanthocarpum'

Compared with most of Europe, Britain has a fairly limited range of native shrubs. These include, however, several which are equal in garden merit to those from China and North America and no better example is there than *Viburnum opulus*, the Guelder rose. Native over a large area from Europe and north-west Africa, east to the Caucasus and parts of central Asia, it is also widely distributed in Britain and Ireland where it favours wet places in light woodland as well as in country hedges and thickets.

Its liking for moist places has earned for it the alternative name Water elder (it was once considered to be a kind of elder hence the sixteenth century Latin name for this shrub *Sambucus montana aquatica*). The name Guelder rose, by the way, more properly belongs to the form 'Roseum' ('Sterile') the snowball tree, with its rounded heads of white becoming pink-tinted, sterile flowers (like a small 'mop-head' hydrangea), which either originated or was commonly cultivated in the Dutch province of Gelderland on the German frontier, sometime in the sixteenth century.

Typical *V. opulus* is a large fast-growing perfectly hardy shrub up to 5m (16ft) high and as much or more across, with pithy stems and paired leaves which are toothed and three- to five-lobed like those of a maple. The flowers are borne at the ends of the branchlets in early summer, the flattened heads of small yellowish white fertile flowers surrounded by large white sterile flowers, the whole resembling a lace-cap hydrangea though not quite so dramatic. These are replaced in autumn by drooping bunches of glistening translucent, red currant-like fruits. Autumn also sees the leaves turning through yellow to a brilliant orange and red before being shed. This is not an entirely reliable characteristic, however, and is dependent on several factors including situation, weather and seedling variation.

Sometimes, birds permitting, the fruits decorate the bare branches for some time after leaf fall. They look good enough to eat but experts consider them worthless (though harmless) as a wild food. On the other hand, an essence prepared from the fresh bark has been used in homoeopathy for the treatment of menstrual pain

Viburnum opulus 'Xanthocarpum'
(**Family:** *Caprifoliaceae)*
Pronunciation: *vee-bur*-num
Meaning: Latin name for the European *V. lantana*
Pronunciation: *op*-ew-lus
Meaning: Latin name for a European maple *Acer opalus* which it resembles in shape of leaf
Pronunciation: zănth-ō-*kar*-pum
Meaning: yellow fruited.

and spasms after birth. Curiously, the fruits of the closely related American Cranberrybush viburnum – *Viburnum trilobum* – are used in that country for preserves and jellies.

For garden purposes there are several excellent selections of *V. opulus* including 'Compactum', free fruiting and only half the size which makes it more suitable for smaller gardens, while 'Notcutt's Variety' is vigorous and even more effective than the wild plant in its fruiting and autumn colour. It is more reliable too. 'Xanthocarpum' is equal to the typical plant in vigour and size but with fruits which ripen to a translucent saffron yellow while at the same time the paler green leaves turn yellow. It is quite distinct and worth a place in any collection of shrubs, its fruits having little attraction for birds.

Although all the foregoing are easily raised from seed the named selections only come true from cuttings which can be taken in summer. Both 'Xanthocarpum' and 'Notcutt's Variety' need plenty of room in which to develop and are best placed either alone in a bed or lawn or, if space permits, in mixed groups when they are most impressive in autumn.

Viburnum opulus
'Xanthocarpum'

- HARDY
- SUN OR HALF-SHADE
- MOST MOIST BUT WELL-DRAINED SOILS
- NEEDS SPACE TO DEVELOP
- ZONES 4–8

WINTER

The garden in winter can be almost as exciting as in spring or summer. With a little thought and imagination, and not a lot of expenditure, you can add just enough winter specials to make it an inviting prospect, where a visit is worthwhile whatever the weather. There are, for instance, a surprising number of shrubs that choose to flower in winter and as many of these are also scented their contribution is invaluable. Just as important are those shrubs whose berries, if not at their peak in winter, at least stay colourful and cheerful. In the same way those deciduous shrubs with coloured shoots are best admired at this season especially if they have been carefully pruned to encourage brighter effect. Backing all these are the evergreens, not the boring kinds that are best seen in specialist collections but those whose habit of growth or foliage colour attracts our attention, inviting closer inspection. With just a sprinkling of these shrubs the winter garden will become a magical place.

Cornus mas

Cornus mas
- HARDY
- SUN OR HALF-SHADE
- MOST SOILS
- ZONES 5–8

While holidaying in Tuscany in 1989 I was struck by the common occurrence in woodlands and thickets there of the Cornelian cherry – *Cornus mas*. From the low hills around Siena to the high ridges of the Monte del Chianti it competed with hazel, hawthorn and sometimes firethorn (*Pyracantha coccinea*) as the dominant understorey to oak and hop hornbeam (*Ostrya carpinifolia*). In its summer green it was hard to distinguish at a distance from the hazel, the two being of similar bushy growth, but on approaching closer the dogwood's smaller, glossier and slender pointed leaves with their distinct venation were immediately apparent.

The sun-drenched hills of the Chianti region, however, seemed light-years removed from my first encounter with this shrub in my home town of Bolton in Lancashire when, as a keen apprentice with the Parks Department, I was brought a mystery twig to identify. It was a crisp February day and yet the twig I held was studded with button-sized clusters of tiny yellow flowers. I had never seen the likes of this shrub before and naturally, I asked to be taken to see it as soon as convenient. It was within easy cycling distance of the park where I worked, growing in an old and neglected private garden. It was a large densely branched twiggy bush of 3m (10ft) and as much across, its branches spreading over the garden wall above the path on which we stood. I could hardly believe my eyes for every twig seemed to be spangled with flower clusters while all else around was lifeless or leafless.

I kept the original twig in a glass of water at home and watched the remaining plump buds expand and burst into flower. Each year since I have endeavoured to pick a well budded twig of *C. mas* to place in my study as a reminder of that first encounter. The flower buds are formed the previous summer and may begin to open in mid or late winter, depending on the weather, continuing into early or even mid spring. Warm weather speeds their development and it is ideal for picking to flower indoors at Christmas.

It is native over a wide area of central and south-east Europe and, in countries enjoying warm summers, regular crops of juicy red fruits are borne. Their taste, however, is sharp and they are best used in making syrups and preserves.

In some years the leaves in autumn turn a rich red or reddish purple before falling, a considerable bonus in any garden. There are also several coloured leaved forms of which 'Variegata' with creamy white margined leaves is the most satisfactory. Indeed, if you are considering planting *C. mas* in your garden you might well choose 'Variegata' and enjoy the benefit of its summer foliage which is among the best of its kind. Either way, you will need to allow plenty of space to accommodate the shrub's ultimate development which may be anything from 5–8m (15–25ft) high and as much or more across depending on growing conditions. As hardy and tough as a hazel, it is amenable to most situations preferring rich but well-drained soils and it is equally happy in full sun or half-shade.

Given its size and early flowering, *C. mas* is best suited to the medium-sized or large garden and sited against a dark or evergreen background to enhance the flowering effect. In Germany I once saw it used as a large formal hedge, the regular pruning encouraging a compact free flowering (and fruiting) habit.

The species may be propagated by seed when available otherwise it can be grown from cuttings taken in summer. The variegated cultivars must likewise be vegetatively propagated.

Cornus mas
(**Family:** Cornaceae)
Pronunciation: *kor*-nus
Meaning: the Latin name for this plant
Pronunciation: mahs
Meaning: male, an epithet used to distinguish a robust species from a more delicate one which was regarded as female.

Previous pages: ***Viburnum opulus* 'Xanthocarpum':** the fruits often continue into winter untouched by birds.

Corylus avellana 'Contorta'

Corylus avellana 'Contorta'
- HARDY
- SUN OR HALF-SHADE
- MOST SOILS
- ZONES 5–8

I am too young to remember the Scottish music-hall singer Sir Harry Lauder as a performer (he died aged 80 in 1950) but I am familiar with his comic and often sentimental Scots songs especially 'Roamin' in the Gloamin''. I also remember (from film and photographs) his spirally twisted walking stick which was as important to his image as was the flexible cane to Charlie Chaplin. Hence my delight on first seeing many years ago *Corylus avellana* 'Contorta' which is sometimes referred to as the 'Harry Lauder's walking stick' plant.

It is an extraordinary sight in winter with its strongly curled and twisted stems sometimes corkscrew-like. The effect is enhanced in mid or late winter when the male catkins expand, hanging like miniature yellow lambstails up to 7cm (2½in) long. Look closely at the twigs and you will see the tiny red styles of the female flowers protruding from small bud-like clusters of brownish-grey bracts. This unusual form of our native hazel was discovered as a sport in a hedge in Gloucestershire in about 1863 and became popular as a curiosity with Victorian gardeners. Not surprisingly, it was included in his collection of plant aberrations known as the 'lunatic asylum' by the late E.A. Bowles at Myddleton House, Enfield, Middlesex and naturally, found its way into most European botanic gardens to tease generations of botany and horticulture students.

Although slower growing and ultimately much smaller than the normal hazel, *C. avellana* 'Contorta' is capable of reaching 3m (10ft) in time and as much across which bars it from the smaller garden. It is almost exclusively a shrub for winter and early spring effect as the rather twisted coarse dark foliage in summer gives the impression of a bad dose of aphid.

Tough and easy on almost any soil, it is propagated by layering or more commonly by grafting onto the type. The drawback with the last method is the presence of strong suckers arising from the stock which need to be removed as soon as they appear otherwise, if neglected, they will eventually swamp Mr Lauder's curious sticks.

***Corylus avellana* 'Contorta'**
(**Family:** Betulaceae)
Pronunciation: *ko*-ril-us
Meaning: from the Greek name *korylos*
Pronunciation: ă-ve-*lah*-na
Meaning: of Avella Vecchia in Southern Italy
Pronunciation: kon-*tor*-ta
Meaning: twisted (the shoots).

Daphne bholua 'Jacqueline Postill'

All of us enjoy a good story, especially if it concerns adventure or romance, and in the case of *Daphne bholua* 'Jacqueline Postill' we have both. In most of its forms, *D. bholua* is a desirable shrub for the winter garden, with richly fragrant flowers lasting for several weeks if not months. The species is native to the Himalayas, especially to Nepal, Sikkim and Bhutan where it is commonly found on forest margins and in clearings.

Our story begins in February 1962 on a mountain ridge known as the Milke Dande in eastern Nepal. An ex-Gurkha major, Tom Spring-Smyth, acting as guide for a group of scientists, smiled

when one of their number commented on the rich fragrance of a shrub flowering beneath the tree rhododendrons – Nepal's national flower. Tom knew the shrub to be *Daphne bholua*, one of his special favourites and valued by the Nepalis for its inner bark which is stripped and used to make a crude parchment-like paper. Sheets of Bholua paper printed with sacred pictures and designs can be bought quite cheaply in Kathmandu shops and markets and are popular souvenirs with western tourists.

Later that day, on a ridge over 3,000m (10,000ft,) high, the major collected three seedlings of this shrub which he carefully wrapped in

Daphne bholua
'Jacqueline Postill'

- HARDY, BUT NEEDS SHELTER
- SUN OR HALF-SHADE
- MOST SOILS BUT PREFERS LIME-FREE
- EVERGREEN
- ZONES 7–8

moss and packed into a bamboo basket. This he sent on the back of a native porter to Dharan, a small town and Gurkha recruitment centre situated on the plains to the south. Having arrived safely, the seedlings were taken post haste by jeep to Calcutta, on the major's instructions where they were transferred to a diplomatic bag and flown home to London and, in particular, Kew Gardens. On being released from quarantine, two of the seedlings were sent to the Major's parents' home in New Milton, Hampshire. They were planted in their garden and although both flourished for a while, one eventually died for reasons unknown.

The remaining seedling grew into a 2m high bush and each winter its leafless branches were illuminated with clusters of star-like white, purple-stained, fragrant flowers. Sometimes flowering would begin in early winter and continue for the next three months. It was propagated and is now available under the name 'Gurkha'.

Another selected seedling called 'Darjeeling', smaller-flowered and evergreen, begins flowering much earlier, usually in late autumn and is still in excellent condition, severe weather permitting, in late winter. There are other seedlings in cultivation collected by the plant hunter Tony Schilling in Nepal which have larger flowers as well as some with deep rose almost red flowers. These will be invaluable to the gardener when they are more readily available.

Already available and one of my ten most favoured shrubs is 'Jacqueline Postill'. It was raised by the Hampshire propagator Alan Postill and named after the love of his life, a New Zealander whom he met at the Hillier Nurseries near Romsey. In 1978 Alan cross-pollinated the flowers of several specimens of 'Gurkha' growing in The Hillier Arboretum and from them gathered a few seeds. Among the seedlings produced was one of exceptional vigour and with evergreen leaves. Planted in his garden, Alan's seedling quickly developed into a bush of erect habit with rose-purple stained flowers which were larger individually than those of 'Gurkha' and in large clusters.

I was given a grafted plant of this seedling, now named 'Jacqueline Postill', in 1983 and planted it in a border by my front door. It currently stands at 3m (10ft.) and flowering normally begins in early winter, continuing into early to mid spring. At its peak, in late winter, it is stunning when the rich fragrance it exudes is commented upon by all visitors, even at night. Only once has my plant been damaged during a severe winter, losing both flowers and foliage. In an average winter it shrugs off cold periods and any damaged flowers are soon replaced by a second crop. Nevertheless, some shelter from cold winds is advisable if *D. bholua* in all its forms is to flourish. A moist but well-drained soil in sun or half-shade will encourage it further.

It can be increased by seed when available and fertile whilst named selections are most usually propagated by grafting. In March 1991 *Daphne bholua* 'Jacqueline Postill' received the ultimate accolade from the Royal Horticultural Society when it was awarded a First Class Certificate.

Daphne bholua
'Jacqueline Postill'
(**Family:** Thymelaeaceae)
Pronunciation: *dăf*-nay
Meaning: the Greek name for *Laurus nobilis*
Pronunciation: *bo*-loo-a
Meaning: from the native name for this shrub, Bholu Swa.

Elaeagnus × *ebbingei* 'Gilt Edge'

- HARDY
- SUN
- MOST SOILS
- EVERGREEN
- ZONES 7–9

Elaeagnus × ebbingei 'Gilt Edge'

For garden purposes, the species of *Elaeagnus* fall into two distinct groups; evergreen and deciduous. Of the evergreen elaeagnus, the most commonly cultivated are the cultivars of the Japanese *Elaeagnus pungens* which was introduced to European cultivation as long ago as 1829 probably by Philipp von Siebold, a German physician in the employ of the Dutch government. It is a robust shrub with stout thorny branches and leathery leaves which are a glossy dark green above and dull silvery beneath. If you examine the undersurface through a hand lens you will see a pelt of starry scales with a scattering of larger brown ones. This scaly coating, which is also found on the shoots and flowers, is common to all elaeagnus though it is more conspicuous on some than others. The clusters of small silvery cream flowers are borne in the leaf axils in mid to late autumn and although normally hidden by the leaves, fill the air around with a rich fragrance.

Much planted in the past it has been for some years superseded by a hybrid *Elaeagnus* × *ebbingei* which originated in Holland in 1928. Seedlings were raised by the late Albert Doorenbos of which six were introduced to the trade in 1939. Only two of these, 'Albert Doorenbos' with large leaves and 'The Hague' with narrower leaves and more upright habit, are presently grown. Both are vigorous and leafy with the usual fragrant silvery cream flowers in autumn and have been much planted as hedges and screens. Unfortunately, one at least has proved susceptible to a wilt disease which effects isolated stems often progressing until the whole bush is infected necessitating removal and burning.

More reliable in this respect and far and away the best variegated elaeagnus of its kind is *E.* × *ebbingei* 'Gilt Edge' which is less vigorous in habit, eventually reaching 2.3m (7ft) by as much across. Its bold pointed leaves are silvery scaly beneath and glossy green above with a striking broad but irregular lemon yellow margin. It was found by head propagator the late Charles Williams, as a sport on a stock plant of *E.* × *ebbingei* in Waterer's Nursery at Bagshot, Surrey in about 1966 and has so far shown no signs of reverting or of disease, wilt or otherwise.

The value of *E. ebbingei* 'Gild Edge' was recognised by the Royal Horticultural Society when it received an Award of Merit in 1971 and a First Class Certificate in 1987.

I cannot mention 'Gilt Edge' without also singing the praises of 'Maculata' which is a cultivar of *E. pungens*. Here the large leaf is a glossy dark green above with a bold irregular splash of gold in the centre, phasing into paler yellow and pale green towards the margins. It is often slow to get started, especially in cold northerly areas or in heavy clay soils but can develop eventually into a large shrub up to 3m (10ft) high and as much across. Its only fault is a tendency to produce green leaved reversions which should be removed as soon as they appear. Reversions, by the way, are encouraged by frequent pruning, so beware of taking too generous a helping of cut material for home decoration. 'Maculata' received a First Class Certificate from the Royal Horticultural Society as long ago as 1891 but its origin is uncertain, possibly Japan.

'Gilt Edge' and 'Maculata' are quite hardy and adaptable to most soils and situations providing these are not too wet. They are especially suited to coastal gardens being tolerant of wind and salt spray so long as it is not too excessive. They make handsome specimens for a large lawn, otherwise they are best planted in a border preferably with a green or dark background. Both these elaeagnus may be propagated by cuttings in late summer or autumn. 'Maculata', certainly, is sometimes grafted by continental nurserymen, a not entirely satisfactory method as the resultant suckers need to be removed completely.

Elaeagnus* × *ebbingei
(**Family:** Elaeagnaceae)
Pronunciation: e-lee-*ăg*-nus
Meaning: a Greek name originally applied to a willow, from *helodes* (growing in marshes) and *hagnos* (pure) referring to the white fruit masses (of the willow)
Pronunciation: e-*bing*-gee-ee
Meaning: after J.W.E. Ebbinge of Boskoop, Holland.

Erica carnea 'Myretoun Ruby'

When my family and I first moved to our present home in Hampshire in 1982 I made an island bed in the lawn in our front garden. Apart from a Kashmir rowan – *Sorbus cashmiriana* with its marble-like white fruits in autumn and early winter – everything else in this bed is low growing. There are dwarf conifers and shrubs as well as small bulbous and perennial plants, most of which are represented as individuals. It is a mixed bag, providing flowers in spring and summer, berries and leaf tints in autumn and interesting foliage throughout the year. It lacked only one thing – winter flower colour. To solve this problem I planted three cultivars of the winter heath *Erica carnea*, which now provide colour in my garden from early winter to spring.

The first of the three to flower is 'King George'. Beginning in early winter the tiny urn-shaped flowers crowding the wiry branches open a dark purple pink over dark green foliage often continuing through until early spring. This cultivar is commonly sold under the name 'Winter Beauty' which, according to some authorities, is quite a different cultivar. In late winter the cultivar 'Springwood White' starts to flower continuing into mid spring. Growth is spreading and the pure white flower spikes are effective against the dark foliage. Like 'King George' this is a reliable and popular winter heath which I remember first planting many years ago when an apprentice with a Parks department in Lancashire.

'Springwood White' has been in cultivation since its discovery by Mrs Ralph Walker of Springwood, Stirling, Scotland who found the original plant growing wild on Monte Carreggio in the Italian Alps. It was put into commerce in 1930 when it was given an Award of Merit by the Royal Horticultural Society, followed in 1964 by a First Class Certificate. It was named 'Springwood' to begin with, a name later changed to 'Springwood White' to distinguish it from 'Springwood Pink', a seedling of the former with purplish pink flowers which occurred in Mrs Walker's garden in 1931. In the opinion of some pundits this has been superseded by 'Pink Spangles', a better grower with larger flowers of a bright deep pink introduced by Treseders Nurseries, Truro, Cornwall in 1966.

The third winter heath in my island bed is one of the very best. It has been called classy, superb, outstanding, all of which are justified and I would not be without it. *E. carnea* 'Myretoun Ruby' is one of the last to flower, from early to mid spring, its dark green foliage ideal backing for the flowers which are reddish brown in bud opening to a rich pink intensifying to a strong wine red. They are borne in dense spikes up to 18cm (7in) long. I have a drift of this heath planted around the low dome of a *Rhododendron yakushimanum* and the contrasting foliage of the two is impressive all year round. 'Myretoun Ruby' was raised around 1960 at Myretoun House, Menstrie, Clackmannan, in Scotland. It was put into commerce in 1965 by the nursery firm of Delaney and Lyle of Alloa and it has been a bestseller ever since.

All these winter heaths are hardy and, unlike most others of their kin, are lime tolerant which is a great bonus for those gardening on chalk or limestone soils. This is not so surprising, however, considering that *E. carnea* in the wild often grows in limestone areas. It is native to the mountains of central and southern Europe (Alps, Apennines, Germany, Yugoslavia and the north-west Balkans) where it is widespread in some locations, growing in coniferous woods and stony places, often in alpine zones. It was first introduced to British cultivation apparently, by the Earl of Coventry in 1763 and I wouldn't mind betting that those first plants had the flesh

Erica carnea
(**Family:** Ericaceae)
Pronunciation: e-*ree*-ka
Meaning: the classical name probably for *E. arborea* the tree heath
Pronunciation: *kar*-nea
Meaning: flesh coloured (the flowers).

Erica carnea
'Myretoun Ruby'

- HARDY
- SUN
- MOST SOILS
- EVERGREEN
- ZONES 5–7

pink flowers of the type. Were he to return today I wonder what the Earl would have to say about the great number and variety of cultivars available to the modern gardener?

Their flowers vary in colour from white through pink to purple and red while there are even cultivars selected for their coloured foliage. Like heathers, the winter heaths are most effective when planted in groups or drifts of five or more. Planted at up to 30cm (12in) apart they will in a few years knit together to form dense carpets or low hummocks which can be kept in trim by an annual clipping of the flower spikes once they start to fade. When in flower they vary between 15 and 20cm (6 and 10in) in height according to the cultivar. Given their small size and compact nature the winter heaths are very versatile in the garden and may be used as ground-cover beneath trees and shrubs or as a feature in their own right with perhaps dwarf conifers and shrubs to add variety and height. They also make excellent trough or container subjects for the courtyard or terrace. They associate particularly well with pines, birch and mountain ash and, naturally, with heathers (*Calluna*) and summer flowering heaths on acid soils.

Apart from rabbits, winter heaths have few enemies. Heather die-back, a soil borne fungal disease which attacks the roots and collar, is an occasional problem and affected plants are best removed and burned. Replacing old worn-out plants, which have become straggly and few flowered, with new ones is a wise policy and considering that they are easily propagated by cuttings in summer or by detaching rooted layers this is worth pursuing. They must also be irrigated in periods of drought.

Hamamelis mollis

The witch hazels are among the most easily recognised and ornamental of all hardy shrubs. I shall never forget my very first meeting with the Japanese species – *Hamamelis japonica* – on a bright but cold winter's day in the early 1950s. With a friend I was exploring a large neglected woodland garden at the foot of Rivington Pike, a well known beauty spot on the moors above Horwich in Lancashire.

Hamamelis mollis
- HARDY
- SUN OR HALF-SHADE
- MOIST, COOL, PREFERABLY LIME-FREE SOILS
- ZONES 6–8

We pushed our way through a thicket of sycamore saplings and snowberry and found ourselves in a clearing in which grew a low wide-spreading shrub. Its branches were studded with clusters of spidery flowers with red bodies and crinkly yellow legs. We hadn't a clue what this curious shrub might be and we were very excited thinking we had found a rare treasure. It was not until we found its picture in a book that we identified it although it was not as rare in cultivation as we had imagined. The flowers of the witch hazels are their greatest claim to fame and appearing as they do in winter, they are doubly welcome.

There are five species in the wild, three in North America and one each in China and Japan. The most famous of the American species and the first of its kind to be introduced to Britain is *Hamamelis virginiana* which was identified by the early settlers with the common hazel (no relation) of Europe and its branches utilised as divining rods to locate the source of underground springs and steams, hence the name witch hazel, i.e. the hazel with magical properties. An essence of witch hazel distilled from the steamed twigs and leaves is still a most effective treatment of bruises whilst another use is in eye lotions. From a nurseryman's point of view the Virginian witch hazel is important as an understock on which to graft the more ornamental cultivars.

From an ornamental standpoint the most attractive flowering witch hazels are from Asia, especially the Chinese *Hamamelis mollis* and its hybrids with *H. japonica* known under the name *Hamamelis × intermedia. H mollis* itself is a native of woodlands in western and central China and was first introduced to British cultivation by the plant hunter Charles Maries in 1879. Curiously, Messrs Veitch, the nurserymen to whom Maries sent his seed, did not recognise this plant for what it was (a new species) believing it to be a form of the Japanese witch hazel. Indeed, the only seedling to appear grew for some years in Veitch's Coombe Wood nursery in Surrey before its true status was recognised and this plant is still available today under the name *H. mollis* 'Coombe Wood'.

Its flowers are golden yellow with a red calyx and are richly fragrant. *H. mollis* was also introduced at a later date by E.H. Wilson and plants derived from his collections are little different and just as ornamental as Maries' introduction. No wonder that it was awarded a First Class Certificate by the Royal Horticultural Society as long ago as 1918. The flower-buds are formed during summer at the base of the current year's growths and begin opening in early or mid winter depending on the weather. If winter is not too severe you can expect flowers to be open for Christmas and cut flowering twigs brought into your home will certainly open at this time.

A fine selection of *H. mollis* is named 'Goldcrest'. It was raised at Bodnant Gardens in North Wales probably from seed collected by Wilson. It differs from the typical plant in its slightly larger flowers, the deep golden yellow petals stained crimson at their base. It is also later flowering, the flowers commonly opening from mid-February when those of the type are on the wane. It received an Award of Merit from the RHS in 1961.

Of the several hybrids of the Chinese witch hazel, *Hamamelis* 'Pallida' is not only the finest but lays strong claim to being the most spectacular of *all* witch hazels. It certainly is the most popular and for good reason. The large flowers with pale sulphur-yellow petals, densely crowd the branchlets from mid to late winter or even earlier and an established bush at this time is little short of sensational. The flowers are scented as a bonus. 'Pallida' was raised in the Royal Horticultural Society's garden at Wisley from seeds probably obtained from the Belgian nursery of Kort at Kalmthout on the Dutch border. It received an Award of Merit in 1932 and a First Class Certificate in 1958. Other hybrids worth growing are 'Arnold Promise' raised at the Arnold Arboretum, Massachusetts and named in 1963. This fragrant cultivar is late in flowering, usually late winter or early spring, while the petals are a clear yellow.

For lovers of the unusual there are several hybrid witch hazels with red or orange flowers. Perhaps the two most worth growing are 'Jelena' with large flowers which from a distance in sunshine glow a bright coppery orange while those of 'Diane' are a uniform rich red. Both are at their best any time between mid winter and early spring and were raised at the Arboretum Kalmthout in Belgium by Robert and Jelena de Belder.

All these witch hazels are strong growing (especially the hybrids) with spreading and ascending branches which make them more suitable for large- or medium-sized gardens where, over many years, they are capable of reaching 5–6m (15–20ft) high and as much or more across. Their leaves are relatively large and rounded, colouring a rich butter yellow before falling in autumn, except in the case of 'Arnold Promise' and the red and orange flowered hybrids which turn red or purplish red. It is worth mentioning that the flowers of these witch hazels last longer in cold weather. The petals appear to be virtually frost proof. Witch hazels are happiest when out of the wind in sun or half-shade and make splendid specimens in woodlands or on large lawns where their full expanse can be accommodated. As for soils, they thrive best in a cool lime-free loam that does not dry out in summer.

Propagation is normally by grafting whilst seed, when available, produces seedlings of variable quality. Layering is also possible.

Hamamelis mollis
(**Family:** Hamamelidaceae)
Pronunciation: hăm-a-*may*-lis
Meaning: Greek name for another plant
Pronunciation: *mol*-lis
Meaning: softly hairy (the young leaves and shoots).

Ilex aquifolium 'Ferox Argentea'

No British garden in winter would be complete without a holly of some kind, preferably the English holly *Ilex aquifolium* or its hybrid (with *Ilex perado*) *Ilex × altaclerensis* known as the Highclere holly. Most of these, however, are trees and out of the compass of this book, but a small number are sufficiently slow growing to be maintained, if desired, as a large bush. Such is the Silver Hedgehog holly *I. aquifolium* 'Ferox Argentea' which has been a favourite of mine since I first saw it 30 years ago in the gardens of Haigh Hall, a private estate turned public park near Wigan in Lancashire.

Left to its own devices, this holly will eventually make a small tree of 6m (20ft) or so but it is easily kept as a medium-sized to large bush by judicious pruning of the new shoots in late summer. Indeed, so useful is it as cut material for the home, especially at Christmas, that there should be no problem in growing this holly in all but the smallest gardens. The leaves are small for an English holly up to 5cm (2in) long, being thick and leathery and wavy. In colour they are dark green with a creamy-white margin while there are short creamy-white spines on both the margins and the upper leaf surface.

The only drawback of 'Ferox Argentea' (if drawback it is) is that being a male form, it bears no berries but this is more than compensated for by the bright and curious foliage which is densely set on contrasting deep purple shoots. It is a charming and amusing holly and makes an ideal gift especially for young gardeners.

'Ferox Argentea' arose as a sport on the more vigorous green-leaved 'Ferox', the Hedgehog holly, which as a matter of interest, is one of the oldest forms of the English holly in cultivation having been grown since the seventeenth century. Given its hardiness and slow growth, the Silver Hedgehog holly can be grown in a wide range of situations but is best seen as a specimen plant in the lawn or else in a bed in the patio or courtyard. For the same reasons it also makes an attractive, if unusual, container plant in sun or shade.

All the English hollies are amenable to most soils so long as they are not waterlogged although a rich well-drained soil suits them best. They may be propagated by cuttings in late summer.

Ilex aquifolium
'Ferox Argentea'
(**Family:** Aquifoliaceae)
Pronunciation: *ee*-leks
Meaning: the Latin name for this plant
Pronunciation: ă-kwi-*fo*-lee-um
Meaning: the Latin name
Pronunciation: *fe*-rox
Meaning: ferocious, very thorny
Pronunciation: ar-*gent*-ee-a
Meaning: silver (the thorns).

Ilex aquifolium
'Ferox Argentea'

- HARDY
- SUN OR SHADE
- MOST SOILS
- EVERGREEN
- ZONES 7–9

Jasminum nudiflorum
- HARDY
- SUN OR SHADE
- MOST SOILS
- ZONES 6–10

Jasminum nudiflorum

The winter jasmine is probably the most popular and easily recognised of all winter flowering shrubs in gardens. This is hardly surprising considering its hardiness, adaptability and reliability. There can be few gardens where this shrub will not grow or a single winter when its flowers do not appear, yet, in an account of shrubs for winter effect it would be churlish to omit this gem whose bright yellow tubular flowers are produced along the green whip-like shoots for months on end. Indeed, the first flowers often appear in late autumn and the last in late winter or early spring depending on the weather. During winter, the slightest rise in temperature will open the red-tinted buds which are produced in such numbers that a new crop is always ready to replace those that fade.

Although some might argue that this is not a shrub, then neither is it a true climber for in gardens, certainly, it needs to be fastened to a support be it a wall, fence or tree stump to prevent it rambling along the ground. In some situations, however, it can be put to good use as ground-cover and I have seen it clothing steep banks and rough, otherwise unproductive, ground with its numerous stems which will root at the tips like a bramble or layer when in contact with moist soil. Its undoubted vigour (its stems can reach 5m (16ft) when trained) is perhaps its only drawback in a small garden, but it can be controlled by judicious and regular pruning, cutting hard back the flowering shoots immediately they are spent in early spring.

Although it is perfectly adaptable to shade and is often seen on a wall facing away from the sun, there is no doubt that the winter jasmine flowers best and most prolifically in a sunny situation. The leaves are composed of three leaflets which in summer provide a

Jasminum nudiflorum
(**Family:** Oleaceae)
Pronunciation: yăs-*meen*-um
Meaning: from *yasmin* the Persian name
Pronunciation: new-di-*flo*-rum
Meaning: flowering naked; it flowers on the leafless shoots in winter.

pleasant glossy green screen. In a wild state the winter jasmine is native to China where it is widely distributed especially in the north and east, occurring in hillside scrub and ravines. It has long been cultivated by the Chinese, however, over a much greater area and is commonly seen in gardens and courtyards in places as far apart as Beijing, Shanghai and Kunming. It was from a Chinese nursery or garden probably in Shanghai that the Scottish plant collector Robert Fortune first introduced this shrub to British cultivation in 1844 and if he had sent back nothing else he would still be remembered with gratitude by gardeners, for no other shrub provides a more cheering sight on a dull and cold winter's day. Even the fact that the flowers are scentless does not detract from their merit.

It can be rooted by cuttings from late summer to the end of the year but any length of shoot, a branch even, if thrust into the ground in late autumn or early winter will invariably take root while a well-established and rampant specimen will produce an endless supply of suckers or layered pieces.

Lonicera × purpusii 'Winter Beauty'

Among the many species of shrubby honeysuckles in cultivation *Lonicera fragrantissima* and *Lonicera standishii* are grown for their masses of small white, richly fragrant flowers in winter. Both are native to China and both were introduced to British cultivation by Robert Fortune in 1845, probably from a Shanghai nursery.

They are large shrubs averaging 2–2.7m (6–8ft) by as much across and are hardy and amenable to most soils in sun or half-shade. Should they become too large or unshapely they can safely be pruned (hard if necessary) in spring. The same applies to the hybrid between the two, *Lonicera × purpusii*, which was raised in the Darmstadt Botanic Garden in Germany sometime before 1920. It is a semi-evergreen shrub, that is the leaves are shed in severe winters, while the creamy-white two-lipped flowers are equal in scent to those of its parents. None of these honeysuckles can be called showy but their flowers are pretty when seen close-to and their fragrance is sweet and pervasive.

In 1966, in his garden at Eastleigh near Southampton, Reg (Alf) Alford, then foreman of Hilliers Eastleigh Nursery, pollinated the flowers of *L. × purpusii* with pollen from *L. standishii* var. *lancifolia*, a narrow leaved form of the type introduced by E.H. Wilson from west China in 1908. From this cross, two seedlings resulted one of which has been introduced to commerce under the name 'Winter Beauty'. From a garden point of view *L. × purpusii* 'Winter Beauty' is similar to the type in most respects but is freer flowering over a longer period from early winter to mid spring. Although warm weather can open a few flowers as early as late autumn, it normally reaches its peak in mid and late winter when every twig is spangled with bloom and the garden is awash with its fragrance.

Lonicera × purpusii
(**Family:** Caprifoliaceae)
Pronunciation: lon-i-*se*-ra
Meaning: after Adam Lonitzer (1528–86), German naturalist
Pronunciation: pur-*pus*-ee-e
Meaning: after Carl Albert Purpus (1853–1941), German plant collector in Central America.

Given its size and lack of interest in summer 'Winter Beauty' is best accommodated in a large bed or border preferably, at the rear to allow for summer planting in front. It can also be grown against a wall and its branches carefully pruned and trained to wires or similar support. If the wall be warm and sunny, better flowering should result. When training this way, remember that flowers are produced on shoots of the previous year so any pruning is best done immediately after flowering, in spring. Propagation is by cuttings in summer or by hard wood cuttings in winter.

Above left: ***Lonicera* × *purpusii***
'Winter Beauty'

- HARDY
- SUN OR HALF-SHADE
- MOST SOILS
- ZONES 6–9

Above: ***Ribes laurifolium***

- HARDY
- SUN OR HALF-SHADE
- MOST SOILS, PREFERABLY MOIST BUT WELL-DRAINED
- EVERGREEN
- ZONES 7–9

Ribes laurifolium

To anyone brought up with the blackcurrant and the gooseberry, *Ribes laurifolium* comes as something of a shock. For a start it is evergreen, and secondly, its greenish yellow flowers are borne in late winter or early spring at least a month before those of the familiar 'Flowering currant' *Ribes sanguineum*. In a genus of mainly deciduous, spring flowering shrubs it is undoubtedly a curiosity but one with assured ornamental appeal.

It is one of the many shrubs I first encountered while a student at the University Botanic Garden, Cambridge and specimens of it regularly appeared in plant identification tests during the winter months. At Cambridge, it grew on the famous limestone rock garden, built by the late Bob Younger, where it formed a low spreading mound of leafy branches under 1m (3ft) high and rather more across. The leaves are smooth and leathery, coarsely toothed, 7.5–10cm (3–4in) or occasionally 12.5cm (5in) long, quite substantial for the size of plant. They are a dull dark green above, paler below and carried on short bristly stalks. The flowers, meanwhile, are borne in nodding clusters (racemes), male and female on separate plants (dioecious)

Ribes laurifolium
(**Family:** Grossulariaceae)
Pronunciation: *rie*–beez
Meaning: from Arabic or Persian *ribas* (acid tasting), referring to the fruit
Pronunciation: low-ri-*fo*-lee-um
Meaning: Laurus-leaved.

and are followed in some years by reddish brown, bristly fruits. Of the two, the male form is the most satisfactory in flower, the clusters being longer – 5cm (2in) – while the individual flowers are larger. Neither is what you might call showy but they possess what enthusiasts call a curious charm.

Introduced to cultivation by E.H. Wilson in 1908, *R. laurifolium* is native to west China in the provinces of Yunnan and Sichuan where it occurs often as an epiphyte on mossy rocks and tree trunks. It was in just such a situation that I saw it in 1981 in the Cangshan, a range of mountains above Dali in western Yunnan. It was climbing a mossy trunk and seemed as happy as a sandboy. It is worth encouraging it to climb a wall, fence or suitable tree in your garden providing conditions are not too dry. Given a wire support it will reach 2m (6ft) where its flowers, as a result, are more conveniently examined.

Given a moist but well-drained situation in sun or half-shade it will grow in most soils even those on chalk. Propagation is by cuttings in late summer or by layering.

Ruscus aculeatus

Anyone fond of walking in the woods of southern and south-east England and south-west Wales may well have come across the Butcher's broom *Ruscus aculeatus*, a dwarf, native evergreen which is usually found as scattered clumps and colonies in well-drained often stony situations. It appears to be tolerant of a wide range of soils and from my home in Hampshire I can visit it in the beechwoods on the chalk hills above Selborne, Gilbert White's village, as well as on the clays of the New Forest.

Whichever way you look at it, it is a curious thing with its strong but flexible green stems and small spine-tipped leathery leaves carried on the many branched head. On checking this plant out, the first thing one learns about it is that these 'leaves' are nothing of the kind and are in reality short, flattened leaf-like stems (called cladodes by botanists), specially modified to do the job of the true leaves which exist as tiny papery scales on the cladode's upper surface. In the axils of the true leaves the minute greenish white flowers are borne in spring, male and female flowers on separate plants. When pollinated, the females produce green fruits that swell to marble size and ripen to a shining sealing-wax red by autumn, lasting for many months and certainly throughout winter. Indeed, although I have read reports to the contrary I have yet to see them being taken by birds.

Tough, hardy and adaptable, there are few garden soils in which the butcher's broom will not grow and it is one of the best woody plants for shade. There are in cultivation free fruiting hermaphrodite forms, that is, plants whose flowers (some at least) are perfect (with fertile male and female parts). Some nurseries offer them as vegetatively propagated progeny.

Ruscus aculeatus
(**Family:** Ruscaceae)
Pronunciation: *rus*-kus
Meaning: the Latin name
Pronunciation: a-kew-lee-*ah*-tus
Meaning: prickly (the leaves).

Ruscus aculeatus

- HARDY
- SUN OR SHADE
- MOST SOILS
- EVERGREEN
- ZONES 8–9

The common name is probably a misnomer as there is no clear evidence that it was ever used by butchers to clean their blocks although in areas where it commonly grows, berried sprigs are said to have been used by some butchers to decorate the huge Christmas sirloins. I have it on good authority that bunches of the prickly branches tied to the end of a long flexible pole were once used by cottagers in the New Forest to clean their chimneys while in the same area it used to be picked by gypsies and sold as a Christmas decoration. I can also confirm from personal experience that a single stem makes an effective fly swat! Propagation is by seed or by division, the latter method being the only means of increasing good berrying forms. This is best accomplished in spring.

Sarcococca hookeriana digyna
- HARDY
- SUN OR SHADE
- MOST SOILS
- EVERGREEN
- ZONES 6–9

Sarcococca hookeriana digyna

It was, I believe, my old director at the University Botanic Garden, Cambridge, the late John Gilmour, who coined the name Christmas box for the sarcococcas. They were among his favourite shrubs and, not surprisingly, were well represented in the Botanic Garden where they had been planted in a special bed underplanted with an equally impressive collection of snowdrops. The nodding white flowers of the latter beneath the dark green of Sarcococcas was a sight many visitors came specially to enjoy and this lesson in plant association was not lost on us students.

There are several species of *Sarcococca* in cultivation, all evergreen and all with axillary clusters of tiny petal-less flowers whose main ornament lies in the stamens which in most species are white. *S. hookeriana* is a native of eastern Himalaya, north Assam and south-east Tibet and was first introduced to cultivation during the last century. It has never, however, been commonly available in the nursery trade, partly, I suspect, because, away from the warmer south and sheltered areas elsewhere its hardiness is suspect. I have it in my garden from a collection made by Tony Schilling in Nepal and it gets better every year, the axils of its narrow willow-like leaves are crowded with sweetly scented flowers in October and late autumn and sometimes again in mid winter.

A more likely reason for its scarcity, however, is the abundance of its Chinese variety *digyna* which is hardier and more dwarf. This variety was introduced to cultivation from western Sichuan by E.H. Wilson in 1908 and is represented in gardens by two forms, one with dark green stems, the other with the young stems, leaf stalks and midribs a dull purple. The latter has been given the cultivar name 'Purple Stem'. It is a free growing shrub sending up from the base erect stems up to 1m (3ft) tall on average but up to 1.5m (5ft) against a wall or in a sheltered corner. It increases gradually by suckering to form dense clumps of flexible shoots clothed with narrow leathery leaves. The flower clusters normally open in mid or

Sarcococca hookeriana digyna
(**Family:** Buxaceae)
Pronunciation: sar-kō-*ko*-ka
Meaning: from the Greek *sarcos* (flesh) and *kokkos* (a berry) referring to the fleshy fruits
Pronunciation: hu-ka-ree-*ah*-na
Meaning: after Sir Joseph Hooker (1817–1911)
Pronunciation: *dı*-gı-na
Meaning: with two styles.

late winter depending on the weather and at this time the flowering sprays are a pretty sight, filling the air around with a sweet scent. They are followed by shining black fruits which, however, in our climate are rarely in sufficient numbers to be noticeable. In 1981 I saw this shrub growing in a wood in the Cangshan, a range of mountains in west Yunnan province in south-west China. Here, it thrived in a relatively dark situation, a characteristic welcomed by those needing plants for a shady site. It is as happy in sun as it is in shade as long as the soil is reasonably moist in summer and is suitable on both lime-free and alkaline soils.

Two other species *Sarcococca confusa* and *Sarcococca ruscifolia* var. *chinensis* are commonly grown for their sweetly scented white flower clusters in winter. Both are dense, low, clump-forming shrubs with numerous arching stems clothed with small privet-shaped, glossy, dark green leaves. They differ most noticeably in the shining black fruits of the former and the red fruits of the latter. A third species *Sarcococca humilis* (S. *hookeriana humilis*) is the smallest of all – up to 60cm (2ft) on average – freely suckering to form in time extensive colonies. The leaves are narrowly oval up to 7.5cm (3in) long, whilst their flowers, appearing in late winter, are characterised by their white stamens with pink anthers. The fruits are black.

All the sarcococcas may be increased from cuttings in autumn or early winter or from rooted suckers or by seed.

Skimmia japonica 'Nymans'

Skimmia japonica is among the most commonly grown of all small evergreen shrubs. It was first introduced to Britain from Japan by Robert Fortune in 1861 and within three years had been awarded a First Class Certificate when exhibited as a fruiting plant before the Royal Horticultural Society. Amazingly, it was another 40 years before gardeners came to realise that the flowers of this shrub are dioecious (male and female flowers on separate plants) and that a male pollinator was required to produce fruits on a female plant. Over the years a good number of selections have been made and some named for their flowering or fruiting qualities, two of which are particularly outstanding.

'Nymans' is a female selection with slender, erect and ascending branches and relatively small pointed leaves. As in other female skimmias the clusters of white flowers in mid spring are less attractive than those of the male but when pollinated they give way to dense clusters of glossy rounded berries which ripen to a bright Turkish red in winter. In fact, they begin to colour much earlier – in autumn – and often stay on the bush to greet the opening of the new flowers in spring. Where and when 'Nymans' originated is something of a puzzle. The name almost certainly refers to Nymans Gardens at Handcross in Sussex but the present head gardener there, David Masters, can find no information relating to this plant nor is

Skimmia japonica
(**Family:** Rutaceae)
Pronunciation: *skim*-ee-a
Meaning: from the Japanese name for this plant
Pronunciation: ja-*pon*-i-ka
Meaning: of Japan.

Skimmia japonica 'Nymans'
- HARDY
- SUN OR HALF-SHADE
- MOST SOILS, PREFERABLY THOSE WHICH DO NOT DRY OUT IN SUMMER
- EVERGREEN
- ZONES 7–9

it mentioned in *A Garden Flora*, a catalogue of the flowers and trees grown at Nymans between 1890 and 1915 compiled by the then owner Leonard Messell.

My first sight of *S. japonica* 'Nymans' was in the 1960s growing in the garden of the late Lionel Fortescue at Buckland Monachorum in Devon, where a group of some three to five plants occupied the end of a border by the front door. They were 60–90cm (2–3ft) in height and of similar width and presented a fine spectacle in fruit. The small leaves and slender stems allow the berry clusters to be seen without hindrance which is not always the case with these shrubs.

'Rubella', on the other hand, is a male cultivar and very distinct it is in its large terminal heads (panicles) of white, yellow anthered and richly fragrant flowers in spring. As a bonus, throughout winter, the entire flower-head – buds and stalks – is a dark purple-red contrasting with the dark green foliage. Compact and dome-shaped when young, it develops a more erect and less shapely habit in later life eventually reaching 1.3m (4ft).

The only disappointment with 'Rubella' is that it is a poor pollinator despite its being commonly planted as such and I would recommend other cultivars such as 'Fragrans' for this purpose. 'Rubella', by the way, is an old cultivar introduced originally to France from a Chinese nursery by Eugene Simon in 1865. Of recent appearance in Holland is a *S. japonica* seedling called 'Rubinetta' which differs from 'Rubella' in its more compact habit, smaller leaves and in its earlier flowering. When this becomes generally available it will most assuredly receive a warm welcome.

Ideally, *S. japonica* and its cultivars thrive best in half-shade and in a fairly deep, moist, not too alkaline soil where their hungry fibrous root system is well supplied with nutrients. They can, however, be grown on lighter soils, even those on chalk, so long as sufficient moisture is available in summer and a plentiful supply of organic mulch supplied. In dry soils exposed to hot sun, these skimmias too easily fall prey to red spider mite and their growth and appearance suffer as a result. Insufficient moisture and exposure to winds and sun also cause an unsightly leaf chlorosis. Providing conditions are satisfactory, *S. japonica* in its best forms is hardy and effective for year round effect. It can be propagated from cuttings taken in autumn or early winter, seed-raised plants being variable in merit.

Stachyurus praecox

In woodlands and thickets in the mountains of Japan, *Stachyurus praecox* is fairly common and among the first shrubs to flower when winter's grip begins to weaken. The stiffly drooping spikes are formed in the leaf axils on the current year's shoots reaching their full development in autumn but not opening until early spring of the following year – earlier in a mild winter. The individual flowers are small and bell-shaped, pale yellow in colour and when an established plant is in full bloom – the leafless reddish shoots hung with row upon row of yellow tassels – it is a heart-warming sight.

Introduced into Western cultivation in 1864 this remains an uncommon species in gardens where it is normally seen as a large shrub wider than it is high. Specimens of 2 x 2.5m (6 x 8ft) are not uncommon while it is capable of twice this in the wild. The slender-pointed leaves are relatively large, up to 15cm (6in) long and boldly veined, occasionally colouring well before falling in autumn. Although lime tolerant, it prefers a rich, cool, acid soil with plenty of humus and seems equally happy in sun or half-shade. In very cold areas it is worth planting against a warm, sheltering wall, training its

Stachyurus praecox
(**Family:** Stachyuraceae)
Pronunciation: stă-kee-*ew*-rus
Meaning: from the Greek *stachys* (a spike) and *oura* (a tail) referring to the slender flower spikes
Pronunciation: *prie*-koks
Meaning: early (flowering).

Stachyurus praecox
- HARDY
- SUN OR HALF-SHADE
- MOST SOILS
- ZONES 7–8

branches to wires, if necessary, to encourage ripening of the summer growths from which the new flower spikes will appear.

Propagation is by cuttings in summer or by seed when available. Occasionally, a particularly fine form with extra long spikes is raised like this one which grows at Knightshayes Court in Devon.

Sycopsis sinensis

For lovers of the unusual *Sycopsis sinensis* is a must. An evergreen member of the witch hazel family, its petal-less flowers more resemble those of the Persian ironwood *Parrotia persica* – dense button-like heads of stamens with orange-red or red anthers ripening to yellow. These are enclosed in dark brown bracts borne in clusters from the axils of the slender pointed leaves which are leathery and boldly veined above. A large shrub of fairly compact habit, it will in time achieve 4–5m (13–16ft) and 3–4m (10–13ft) across. It is best suited to the medium-sized or large garden planted in an easily accessible position so that its curious flowers can more easily be seen.

These flowers I remember clearly from my student days at the University Botanic Garden, Cambridge. At least once each winter a flowering sprig of *Sycopsis* would be included in plant identification tests and woe betide anyone who did not remember its name. There was a fine bush in the Botanic Garden and I found another peeping over a high garden wall in the nearby village of Grantchester not far from the Old Vicarage of Rupert Brooke fame. Both were planted in a moist but well-drained lime-free soil where they flourished,

Sycopsis sinensis
- HARDY, BUT NEEDS SHELTER FROM COLD WINDS
- SUN OR HALF-SHADE
- MOIST BUT WELL-DRAINED LIME-FREE SOILS
- EVERGREEN
- ZONES 7–9

flowering in late winter and early spring, or earlier in mild winters.

In the wild this shrub is a native of central China in east Sichuan, north-west Hunan and west Hubei where it grows in ravines and rocky places especially near streams. It was in just such a ravine that I saw it in May 1988 when visiting the Baofenghu Lake in the Wulingyuan mountains of north-west Hunan. Here it grew in moist shade, sprouting from crevices in the damp rock face.

In British cultivation it is reasonably hardy so long as it is given a warm situation sheltered from cold winds. In cold inland areas, woodland shelter or that from a wall is normally required. It was first introduced from China in 1901 by E.H. Wilson who thought sufficiently highly of it to include it in his book *Aristocrats of the Garden*. It can be propagated by cuttings in early and mid autumn.

Sycopsis sinensis
(**Family:** Hamamelidaceae)
Pronunciation: si-*kop*-sis
Meaning: from the Greek *sykon* (a fig) and *-opsis* indicating resemblance
Pronunciation: si-*nen*-sis
Meaning: of China.

Viburnum × bodnantense 'Dawn'

One of the loveliest of winter-flowering shrubs is *Viburnum farreri* which used to be known as *Viburnum fragrans*, an apt name considering the rich fragrance of its blooms. It is native to Gansu (formerly Kansu) province in north-west China where it grows in hillside thickets often on the sides of roads and trails. It is also much cultivated there in gardens and has been for a very long time. Curiously, according to the Chinese Flora, the pink flowered form of *V. farreri* is only known in cultivation whilst the wild plant is white flowered, var. *candidissimum* perhaps?

Its introduction is sometimes attributed to Reginald Farrer who, with William Purdom, collected its seed during their 1914–16 Gansu expedition. It was certainly Farrer who, through his writings helped make it more widely known and grown. It was William Purdom, however, who, on a previous expedition to Gansu in 1909–11 first found *V. farreri* in a temple garden in Minchow (now Min Xian) and seeds he then collected were germinated by Messrs Veitch at their Coombe Wood nursery in Surrey. Plants from these seeds found their way into gardens shortly after.

V. farreri is hardy and easy in cultivation, freely producing its sweetly scented pink-tinted white flowers anytime from early winter onwards though it normally reaches a peak in mid and late winter. There are also several forms sometimes available of which the most desirable are var. *candidissimum* with white flowers and 'Farrer's Pink' with flowers of a rich pink. Flowering later in winter and likewise possessed of richly fragrant flowers is the east Himalayan *Viburnum grandiflorum* which differs also in its larger flowers (hence the name) and its more robust, relatively gaunt habit. Unfortunately, its young growths are more prone to frost damage in spring and it needs a sheltered position if it is to thrive.

The potential of these two species combined in a hybrid occurred to a number of imaginative gardeners, one of whom was Frederick Charles (F.C.) Puddle (1877–1952) one time head gardener to Lord

Viburnum × *bodnantense* 'Dawn'

- HARDY
- SUN OR HALF-SHADE
- MOST SOILS
- ZONES 5–8

Aberconway at Bodnant, North Wales and the first of three generations to hold this important post. According to his son Charles Edwin (C.E.) Puddle, who made the cross at his father's suggestion, young plants of the two species were boxed up and kept under glass during the winter of 1933/34. Because of its proven hardiness, *V. farreri* was used as the mother parent while *V. grandiflorum* had to be forced into bloom to provide the necessary pollen which, apparently, is more freely borne in this species. Some 25–30 seeds were produced from the cross of which approximately 16 germinated, the seedlings eventually being lined out in the nursery.

Charles, the son, did not see these plants flowering until 1941 while on leave from His Majesty's forces. His father showed him two seedlings with flowers of a deeper pink than the others and the best of these was eventually planted out in a special bed in the garden. His next memory is of returning to Bodnant after the war in 1946 when the selected seedling had grown into a large free-flowering bush. It was shown before the Royal Horticultural Society in 1943 when it received a Preliminary Commendation and on being shown again in 1947, received an Award of Merit.

The cultivar name 'Dawn' was given in 1950 in which year it was featured in the prestigious *Botanical Magazine*. The transference of pollen from one parent to another, Charles tells me, was made with the aid of a brush from a child's paint-box. The tubular star-shaped flowers of 'Dawn' are borne in crowded clusters on short twigs and spurs along the stems and branches. Individually, they are a rich pink in bud, the colour draining away slightly from the lobes as the flowers mature. A large bush in full flower appears a richer pink from a distance due to the presence of numerous unopened buds.

In habit, 'Dawn' has inherited the stout stems and open branching of the *grandiflorum* parent rather than the denser, more slender stemmed *farreri*. It is capable of reaching 3m (10ft) or more and as much across eventually and such specimens in full flower are very impressive. The leaves are of no special merit although they are bronze on emerging and sometimes colour purplish or purplish bronze before falling in autumn. It requires no special treatment and seems happy in most soils either in sun or half-shade. Usually planted with other shrubs in a border, it also makes a useful informal hedge where space permits or as a specimen in a large lawn.

There are two other cultivars of *Viburnum* × *bodnantense* in general cultivation named 'Charles Lamont' and 'Deben'. The former is named after the late Charles Lamont, one time assistant curator at the Royal Botanic Garden Edinburgh who made the cross in 1932/33, a year before the Bodnant one. Four seedlings resulted none of which, apparently, Lamont considered sufficiently distinct and he neither named nor propagated them. The one which now bears his name is considered by its fans as superior to 'Dawn' in its slightly larger flowers of a more glowing pink in bud. It also begins flowering later in the season, usually mid winter.

The intense pink in 'Charles Lamont' is derived from the *grandiflorum* parent used, an exceptional seedling derived from the collection made by R.E. Cooper in Bhutan in 1914 under his number 3023.

Quite different is 'Deben' (pronounced 'Deeben') a seedling which occurred by chance in the Woodbridge nursery in Suffolk of Messrs Notcutt in the 1950s. It is named after the river on which Woodbridge stands. According to John Dyter of Notcutts, its enduring characteristics include an early flowering period (mid winter to spring) and freedom of flower. The individual flowers are larger than those of 'Dawn', pink-tinted in bud mainly on the lobes, opening apple blossom pink and quickly maturing to white. The white flowers suggest that *V. farreri* var. *candidissimum* was involved while their size shows the influence of *V. grandiflorum*.

Viburnum* × *bodnantense
(**Family:** Caprifoliaceae)
Pronunciation: vee-*bur*-num
Meaning: the Latin name for *V. lantana*
Pronunciation: bod-nant-*en*-see
Meaning: of Bodnant, where the most popular cultivar of this hybrid was raised.

Both the above are of similar height, eventually reaching 3m (10ft) or so. Famous for their winter flower and fragrance, all forms are worth planting within easy range of the house for convenience. So free flowering are they, that flowers spoiled by frost are normally replaced by fast developing buds, providing flowers over a period of many weeks. However, only in a severe frost are the flowers likely to be completely devastated.

These shrubs are easily propagated from cuttings in summer while seeds which are rarely freely produced in Britain will give rise to seedlings of variable merit.

Viburnum tinus 'Eve Price'

Twenty years ago I made my first visit to Spain and there experienced for myself the rich diversity of plant life which thrives on the dry sun-drenched hills of the interior. I was delighted to see rosemary and lavender growing wild and to walk through groves of squat Holm oak (*Quercus ilex*), their fallen leaves crackling underfoot. A few years later I explored similar situations in the South of France and later still in Italy and Greece, and through all these travels I became familiar with those fascinating zones of Mediterranean vegetation the garigue and the maquis. Their very names bring back memories of spiny leaves and rich aromas, crowded gullies and stony places plastered in spring with colourful flowers.

One of the many familiar shrubs found in these places, often as an understorey in woods, is the laurustinus (*Viburnum tinus*) and considering its liking for the good life it never fails to surprise me that this handsome evergreen should deign to grow in the less favourable conditions pertaining in cool temperate climates. Yet, except for consistently cold areas, grow it does and in some situations flourishes to such an extent that it seeds around and is threatened with weed status. The most useful thing about this shrub, apart from its dense evergreen nature, is its extended flowering period. The white flowers are formed in dense flattened terminal heads in late summer and may begin blooming in late autumn. From then on they open in succession throughout the winter months until early or mid spring.

Until fairly recently I would have said that their only drawback was a lack of scent and then I read somewhere that scent was indeed present though not always apparent to the untrained nose. I sniffed them again and yes, there it was, faint yet sweet. Since then I have most often detected it borne on the air on a calm, sunny day. Typical *V. tinus*, often represented in cultivation by the cultivar 'French White', is a robust shrub capable of reaching 4–5m (12–15ft) and as much across when sheltered, even higher in woodland.

Far better for garden purposes and particularly recommended for smaller gardens is the cultivar 'Eve Price' which was named after his wife by the late Sir Henry Price in whose garden, Wakehurst Place

Viburnum tinus
(**Family:** Caprifoliaceae)
Pronunciation: vee-*bur*-num
Meaning: the Latin name for *V. lantana*
Pronunciation: *teen*-us
Meaning: the Latin name.

in Sussex, the original plant grew. It had been planted apparently by the previous owner Gerald Loder who purchased it as a seedling from Messrs Dickson of Chester. It was given its name in 1961 when Sir Henry exhibited cut material before the Royal Horticultural Society who gave it an Award of Merit.

'Eve Price' differs from typical *V. tinus* in its neater, more compact habit, smaller leaves and most strikingly, in its neater flower-heads which are deep red in bud considerably extending their ornamental effect. 'Eve Price' is also in my experience, more generous with its berries particularly in a good summer. Although small, they are an attractive indigo blue ripening to black, quite striking on their red stalks against the green foliage. Similar to 'Eve Prince', but if anything more compact and with neater foliage is 'Pink Prelude'.

Although thriving best in a warm preferably sunny and sheltered situation, laurustinus is surprisingly adaptable and will grow in the shade of trees though it is generally looser habited and less free flowering there. It is also amenable to most garden soils including those on chalk or limestone.

In terms of frost hardiness it is variable, some forms such as 'Eve Price' being more reliable in this respect than others. This cultivar is certainly the one I would recommend for gardens away from warmer areas. Should its foliage be shrivelled by freezing winds it will normally break into new growth from the older wood once winter departs. By the same token, poorly shaped plants and specimens which break apart in maturity may be rejuvenated by hard pruning which is best done after flowering in late spring or early summer.

Propagation is most easily achieved by cuttings any time from late summer to early winter.

Viburnum tinus 'Eve Price'

- HARDY, BUT MAY NEED SHELTER IN CONSISTENTLY COLD AREAS
- SUN OR HALF-SHADE
- MOST SOILS
- EVERGREEN
- ZONES 8–11

Growing Shrubs

Most common, hardy shrubs are relatively easy to grow requiring no particular soil preparations or after-care. Thus forsythias, weigelas, spiraeas, berberis, cotoneasters and many others can be seen flourishing in gardens of all shapes, sizes and soils. There is no doubt, however, that the more suitable the conditions the better the results, be it in growth, foliage, flower or fruit. Attention to certain basic requirements can make all the difference to a shrub's performance while in the case of some shrubs it can be the difference between life and death. The most important considerations in growing shrubs successfully are soil requirement, aspect, ultimate size, frost hardiness and desired effect, not necessarily in that order.

Soils

There is no such thing as a soil perfect for all shrubs, not even the deep rich loam often recommended but which few of us possess. Having said that, there is no question that extremes of soil are generally to be avoided and if you are unlucky enough to have such a soil then you should either make the best (or most) of it or set about improving it. The sort of extremes I have in mind are heavy, badly drained soils and those which dry out in summer. Soils too wet, too dry or too hard or rocky spell trouble and if a wide and interesting selection of shrubs is envisaged then such soils need to be improved before planting.

Soils that are badly drained, especially those that are wet (waterlogged) in summer, will support certain willows and a few other shrubs but will need draining if the range is to be extended. This can be achieved by one or a combination of several methods including open trenches (ditches), drainage pipes or tiles, French stone drains, etc. Mound planting is also worth considering in soils which are wet or liable to seasonal waterlogging. This consists of planting the shrub above ground level in a mound of soil. Likewise, hard or compacted soils will need breaking up and attention paid to drainage. Conversely, dry soils need help to improve their moisture retention be it from the digging-in of organic material (compost, leaf mould, well rotted manure, etc.), a regular mulching or both. Clay soils are considered by many gardeners to be a big problem but they are one of the most fertile of soils and once the drainage has been improved they will promote good growth. If it is possible to apply lime to clay soils most will show improved drainage characteristics. This is not recommended, however, if lime-hating shrubs are to be grown.

ACID OR ALKALINE

At my previous home in Winchester, Hampshire I gardened on a chalk marl which was very stony (mainly flints) and when wet very sticky and difficult to work. It enjoyed (if enjoyed is the word) a pH of about 8 (neutral is 7). With liberal helpings of manure and compost I found I could grow a wide range of shrubs including most flowering deciduous kinds – lilacs, deutzias and philadelphus (mock orange) in particular thrived – while the winter flowering heaths – cultivars of *Erica carnea* and *Erica × darleyensis* were excellent value. I could not, however, grow the common heather *Calluna vulgaris* and its numerous cultivars, nor my favourite rhododendrons and azaleas, gaultherias and pieris nor all those other lovely and fascinating members of the *Ericaceae* (Erica family) that abhor lime in the soil. And it wasn't only *Ericaceae*. Camellias, many of the loveliest magnolias, as well as fothergillas and clethras prefer their soils on the acid side and at best grow indifferently with often chlorotic foliage on those of an alkaline nature.

If I were to choose an ideal soil it would be one where the reading is between 5 and 6, certainly below neutral. But for all those who garden on alkaline soils there is the option of growing their favourite 'lime haters' in specially prepared composts (sometimes advertised as ericaceous composts) in tubs or raised beds. These are far preferable in the long term to a sunken bed lined with plastic and filled with ericaceous or peaty compost which always seems eventually to deteriorate or spring a leak and let the lime in. Watering with 'hard' water from a tap is not likely to cause problems, at least in the short term, and can always be counteracted with a granulated pine-bark mulch or similar. Rain-water, of course, is the ideal answer. Given that the future use of peat as a soil conditioner and mulch is at best uncertain it behoves gardeners to try the various alternatives presently on the market. No doubt others will follow. Before using these, however, especially with lime-hating plants, you should first check their pH rating. Some of them have too high a pH to be used with the likes of rhododendrons, azaleas and camellias, though they may otherwise be suitable as a soil conditioner. Granulated pine-bark is an acceptable substitute for peat in these circumstances.

Camellia japonica **'Donckelaarii'** demands a lime-free soil.

Aspect

LIGHT AND SHADE

Shrubs, like all green-leaved plants, need light in order to survive. This does not mean, however, that they all demand a position in full sun. True, there are many shrubs especially those from Mediterranean regions such as cistus, fremontodendron and grevillea, that grow and certainly flower best where sunlight and warmth are available for much of the day. Conversely, there are shrubs which tolerate, if not prefer, some shade so long as moisture is available in summer. But by far the majority grow best in a situation open to the sky.

Sun can ripen growth and encourage more abundant flowering and fruiting while in times of drought it can be a curse, drying out the soil and with it the roots, causing wilting, poor growth or even death.

In deciding where to place a shrub it is helpful to know where it comes from in its native state. Those that favour woodland situations in cool climates will be the least tolerant of hot sun or drought in the garden. Shrubs from the warmer, sunnier hills and woodland margins of southern Europe and similarly Mediterranean climates will, as one would expect, be more tolerant of a baking. Availability of moisture in times of drought is perhaps the most critical factor in a shrub's survival. Light shade or a generous mulching are important factors in reducing water loss.

EXPOSURE

Just as much a problem as the sun's heat in causing water loss from the soil surface and the leaf is exposure to drying winds. There are, of course, varying degrees of exposure and if other agents such as pollution or salt spray are involved, then the effect on a shrub can be much more serious. Fortunately, to take the salt problem first, there are a good number of shrubs including olearias, elaeagnus, hebes and the mop-head hydrangeas, which, within reason, are tolerant of sea wind and salt spray as can be seen in any maritime area. Pollution, too, of the industrial smoke and exhaust variety is tolerated by a surprising number of the more common shrubs but, obviously in the long term, is not a satisfactory or acceptable situation.

As for pure, unadulterated wind, shrubs such as heathers and heaths and dwarf rhododendrons which thrive in the wild on such rigorous fare will not give a jot, but for most shrubs, shelter of some kind is conducive to healthy and balanced growth. Some shrubs – many of the thin-leaved Japanese maples for instance – abhor cold winds and draughts and depend on the protection of other shrubs and trees for their best performance. Windbreaks, either natural or manufactured, may be the only answer to serious exposure and there are a variety of trees, shrubs and conifers suitable

Ultimate Size

Most shrubs have a known size range and, within reason, it is possible to estimate the likely size of a shrub on a given site. Factors such as soil, aspect and exposure all have an effect on the finished result but on the whole there should be no difficulty for an expert in estimating a shrub's growth potential.

Being something of a collector, my garden of 1/4 acre is packed with plants and providing suitable sites for new arrivals is no easy task, yet it is curious how many people with larger gardens and plenty of space still end up planting shrubs in the wrong places.

In the wild, shrubs commonly grow in close packed communities where competition is fierce. A typical hillside in the mountains of western China, for instance, might have philadelphus, roses, buddlejas, deutzias, shrubby honeysuckles, rhododendrons, hypericums, spiraeas and berberis all

Halimium **'Susan'** is an excellent sun-loving drought-tolerant shrub.

Opposite: *Cistus* **'Peggy Sammons'** brings a touch of the Mediterranean to the garden.

cheek by jowl. In a garden situation this wild crush is not practical except in special circumstances and in smaller gardens, certainly, shrubs are more commonly planted and enjoyed for their individual, rather than their massed effect.

Planted in close groups of like kind, shrubs will usually unite to form in time a single clump or mound. Planted in dense mixed groups shrubs tend to grow taller and produce eventually a showy face without much 'bottom'. That is, the lower branches of the shrub will either have died or become entangled in those of its neighbours and the flowers or fruits will all be borne on the top or on the face of the shrub exposed to the light. If a shrub is worth buying and growing for its ornamental effect then it is worth giving it as much elbow room and light as possible to encourage a rich and regular performance. Shrubs grown against a protective wall by the way, will commonly grow to twice or more the size of a free-standing specimen of the same kind.

Frost Hardiness and Drought Tolerance

Between them, frost and drought have in the last decade caused more losses among garden shrubs than from anything else. The majority of shrubs lost or damaged during recent gales in Britain, by the way, have been as a result of trees or boughs falling on them. But droughts, although potentially serious, can be combatted by thorough soil preparation before planting, the regular use of mulching and as a last resort by watering. The dangers of frost, however, are not so easily dealt with. Frozen top soil is bad enough but when this is accompanied by freezing winds the consequences, to evergreens especially, can be dire.

Those living in traditionally milder areas are in theory better off than the rest of us but even there, as winters not long past have proved, one is likely to 'catch a cold' when least expected. I shall never forget the devastation wreaked in 'soft' gardens such as Tresco Abbey and the Ventnor Botanic Garden during the 1986/87 winter. Even my garden in Hampshire which a Swedish visitor once exclaimed 'must be in the banana belt' suffered considerable damage in three winters (1984 to 1987) and not all the plants which suffered were considered frost tender.

Even more of a problem, because they strike at the most critical times, are late spring frosts. Most gardeners have experienced the heartbreak of seeing the newly emerged growth of some favourite shrub destroyed this way. In some cases the damage is so severe that a shrub fails to recover. There have been occasions also when a second flush of growth has been killed by another later frost, adding salt to the wound.

Wherever you garden there are certain basic rules on the cultivation of frost tender shrubs or those of borderline or unknown hardiness:

1 Never plant in known frost pockets.
2 Never plant in damp or badly drained soil.
3 Wherever possible plant in a position sheltered by a wall or by shrubs or trees.
4 Never plant too young or too fragile.
5 Never plant direct from a warm environment such as a heated greenhouse. Give such plants aperiod of 'hardening off'.
6 Plant from a container in early summer when dangers of frost have passed.
7 Don't apply rich feeds in autumn otherwise the resultant late growth will fail to ripen and be damaged.
8 Where practical, establish a reserve stock from cuttings taken in summer and overwintered in a heated or at least a frost-free greenhouse or frame.
9 Keep abreast of local weather forecasts so that, when serious frost is expected, you can provide temporary protection for your more vulnerable shrubs. It is often enough simply to cover the shrub with a thin blanket or polythene sheet.

Killer temperatures result from either radiation frosts or freezing winds. The first of these happens when the surface of the ground, be it a soft or a hard surface, radiates (loses) heat to space leaving the surface colder than at higher levels. Freezing winds are bad enough but when coupled with radiation frosts they can result in very low temperatures (the so-called 'wind-chill' factor).

In order to reduce the damage such conditions can cause, it is worth providing temporary protection to any shrub, especially an evergreen known or suspected of being frost tender. This is certainly worth considering where rare or otherwise important shrubs are concerned. Windbreaks using canes and plastic mesh can be useful in protecting beds or borders while individual protection is worth considering in the case of isolated plants. A simple framework of canes wrapped around with white polythene sheeting or, even better, plastic wind protection netting is normally satisfactory while a cocoon of straw or bracken around the base of the shrub will help protect the rootstock. It is important when protecting shrubs individually to remember that the objective is not to wrap up the entire shrub like a parcel.

Planting Shrubs

Having decided on a shrub for your garden and considered its special requirements, if any, the next most important job is to prepare the site. A good start in life is as important to a shrub as it is to a child and its benefit will be enjoyed for many years to come.

If a shrub border or bed is contemplated then the area chosen should be well dug and a liberal amount of compost or similar organic material incorporated. If the area chosen is close to or incorporates a tree, take great care not to damage or sever major roots which by the way, are closer to the surface than you think. I still have great faith in farmyard (horse) manure and so long as it is 'top quality' and has been well weathered there is none better. Some old hands will claim that such manure is not what it used to be and depending on the source there is some truth in that. I have seen some samples that consisted more of straw than manure with 'gravy' certainly but little or no 'meat', nor is pig or chicken manure an ideal substitute though cow manure is all right when dried and crushed. Pig and chicken manure, by the way, are too high in free ammonia to be risked near delicate roots and foliage. Even horse manure, used fresh, can cause damage by scorching. On the subject of composts, don't use spent mushroom compost which contains chalk if it is intended to plant lime-hating shrubs. Compost made from garden and kitchen vegetable refuse is an excellent source of organic material. It should be composted for at least one year before use.

When planting a shrub border or bed remember to leave plenty of space between individuals to allow for subsequent growth and spread. If the empty spaces in the meantime irritate you then plant them with low growing perennials, bulbs, etc. Such ground-cover can be moved if necessary before the shrubs begin to grow together or else left as a permanent show in which case the shrubs may need to be curtailed by selective pruning.

Shrubs planted as specimens in grass should have a hole dug wider and deeper than the rootball. For instance, a rootball with a 30–45cm (1–1½ft) spread and depth should have a hole dug 60–90cm (2–3ft) wide and 45–60cm (1½–2ft) deep. This will provide plenty of space for the roots to be accommodated without recourse to bending or breaking as well as offering ready access to rainwater. It will also allow space for the addition of compost or similar. Shrubs planted in holes too small suffer root restriction, if not damage, and also act as a sump for excess moisture especially during heavy or continuous rain and in heavy or compacted ground.

However the shrubs arrive, or are purchased, whether it is with their roots bare, balled and wrapped in sacking or polythene (as in evergreens) or in a container, they should be planted as soon as possible during a spell of 'open' weather. Avoid planting when the ground is wet and sticky. On a cold windy day be especially careful to avoid exposing their roots to the drying effects of the wind which can damage, if not kill them in a surprisingly short time.

If the soil excavated from the hole is in any way unsuitable (heavy clay, etc.), it is worth improving it with compost, crushed bark, well-rotted manure or similar. A handful of a general fertilizer mixed in at the same time is also beneficial. Any turf removed at the start of the operation can be turned grass downwards and placed at the bottom of the hole. This in time will rot and provide a useful source of organic matter to the growing shrub. Indeed, according to some authorities, rotting turf provides the *best* source of organic matter, far longer lasting than manure.

Whatever its origin, whether from container or open ground, the shrub should be planted so that at the final stage its topmost roots lie just below the soil surface. When replacing the soil, firm gently with the hands or feet to secure the rootball against rocking in the wind. If necessary, protection against browsing animals especially rabbits, hares and deer can be given by use of chicken wire or one of the many plastic guards available for the purpose.

After-Care

As with all newly planted subjects, shrubs need continuing attention if they are to thrive and perform well. In the first summer, at least, attention must be given to watering especially during periods of warm dry weather. Areas of bare soil in shrub beds and borders or around the base of shrubs planted as specimens in grass must be kept free of weeds. This may be helped by the application of a 2–5cm (1–2in) layer of crushed bark as a mulch. A layer of black plastic is an equally effective, if less attractive, method of preventing weed growth. A successful mulch will also help keep the top soil moist in times of drought or persistent wind.

Some shrubs, once established, appreciate an occasional boost from the application of a general fertilizer. This is especially beneficial if growth is slow, extension growth short, leaf colour pale and the leaves below normal size. Shrubs which are regularly hard pruned to encourage strong new growths, e.g. *Cornus stolonifera* 'Flaviramea', *Rubus bicolor, Buddleja davidii*, etc. benefit greatly from additional feeding. Usually a good handful sprinkled around the drip line beneath the shrub is sufficient, taking care not to leave the fertilizer at the base of the stem or on the leaves and to wash it into the soil should rain fail to appear. This is best applied during maximum growth in spring.

PRUNING

Despite what some people seem to believe, not all shrubs require regular pruning. Indeed, given space and light, shrubs that do benefit from this operation are in the minority. There are two main reasons why pruning is sometimes necessary or desirable; one is to curb or control the growth of

A naturally dwarf shrub requiring no pruning.

fast growing subjects that are getting too large for their allotted space. Pruning of shrubs which have outgrown their space can be attempted almost any time, although I prefer to do it in summer when there is still active growth and when the wounds will heal before winter sets in. Summer pruning also has most influence in reducing vigour. If it is a summer-flowering shrub pruning can be left until immediately after flowering.

Don't be faint-hearted once you have decided to curtail a shrub's growth this way, snipping bits and pieces from the ends of the branches. The best method is to prune whole or part branches back to a bud or secondary branch leaving a good clearance between the shrub and its neighbours.

The other main reason for pruning is to encourage a greater production of flowering or coloured barked shoots for maximum ornamental effect. Thus, shrubs grown for their coloured winter stems such as *Cornus stolonifera* 'Flaviramea' and *Rubus bicolor* can be cut back to within 5–7.5cm (2–3in) of the ground in late winter or early spring in order to encourage the production of strong new shoots for next winter's enjoyment.

As for those shrubs whose flowering performance is increased by annual pruning, these fall into two main groups depending on flowering habit. The first group flower in spring or early summer on shoots developed the previous year. Pruning, if decided upon, consists of cutting back these shoots, or at least a proportion of them, to within one or two buds of the base immediately flowering has finished. Shrubs in this group include *Buddleja globosa* (but not *B. davidii*), *Weigela, Philadelphus, Deutzia, Tamarix parviflora, Prunus fruticosa, Cytisus scoparius* and hybrids and *Forsythia*.

The second group of shrubs meanwhile, flower on the current year's shoots usually in late summer or autumn. Here pruning consists of cutting the old shoots back to within two or three buds of their base in late winter or early spring. Shrubs of this group include *Buddleja davidii, Hydrangea paniculata, Spiraea japonica, Caryopteris, Perovskia, Romneya* and hardy fuchsias (unless grown as a hedge).

Flowering shrubs such as *Hypericum* can be hard or lightly pruned in late winter or early spring, depending on available space. In my plantsman's garden, for instance, I need to grow numerous shrubs as well as trees, annuals and perennials. Consequently, without pruning, things would soon develop into a jungle. Most of my hypericums, therefore, and I have fifteen different kinds, I cut hard back each year which guarantees me a colourful display on bushes of manageable size.

Some shrubs, such as heathers and heaths (*Calluna* and *Erica*), can benefit from an annual or biennial clipping to remove the old flowering shoots immediately after flowering.

Pests and Diseases

In a book of this nature I can do no more than point out a few of the most commonly encountered pests and diseases of shrubs.

Pests

Aphids (greenfly and blackfly), of which there are numerous species, may affect most shrubs at some stage in their development though they are commonly found on the succulent young growths in spring and summer. The main damage caused by their feeding is most often seen *after* their handiwork when growth is stunted and the leaves curl unnaturally or become puckered or discoloured. Similar symptoms occur with scale insects which suck sap from leaf or bark from beneath a protective brownish scale or shell. Leaves finely peppered with pale spots or else yellowed and falling prematurely is often the result of an attack by red spider mites which, despite the name, are variable in colour and particularly active in prolonged dry summers. Whiteflies, which look like tiny white moths, also feed on sap and characteristically rise up in clouds when disturbed. More often than not the above pests when feeding on leaves congregate on the undersides and are therefore hidden.

There are also a range of leaf-eating pests, many of them caterpillars of moths and sawflies as well as weevils, the most notorious of which, the vine weevil, feeds on camellia, rhododendron, azalea and hydrangea, to name a few. Young shrubs and seedlings are sometimes liable to slug damage, especially in damp conditions, and their feeding is not necessarily restricted to the leaves as they will even gnaw tender young bark and roots. Bullfinches can also be a nuisance in some areas nipping out the flower buds of a wide range of shrubs such as *Forsythia, Prunus* and *Ribes* in late winter or spring.

A more obvious source of injury to shrubs is that caused by mammals especially by deer, hares and rodents. This mostly takes the form of young shoots eaten, bark gnawed or rubbed away and, in the case of cats, bark of clear stems scratched.

PEST CONTROL

Increasingly today, there are available biological controls for insect pests whereby predatory agents are introduced to feed on them. However, although these have been used successfully on a commercial scale under glass for some years they are not generally easy for the amateur gardener to apply out of doors though this may well change in the future.

Until such time that all garden pests can be controlled biologically you would be wise to combine such of these controls as are available and appropriate with good cultural practices and a minimum use of pesticides to protect your shrubs. The responsible and sensible use of modern pesticides should present no danger to the user or the environment and provide an economical and reasonably easy way to maintain the health and vigour of your shrubs. There are, however, a number of so called 'bio friendly' pesticides now becoming available, such as aphicides which kill aphids without harming ladybirds or other natural predators.

Before using pesticides of any kind it is absolutely essential that the manufacturer's instructions as to their use, particularly concerning safety precautions, are read, understood and adhered to. To guide you in the range of pest, disease and weed controls available and their safe and effective use I can do no better than recommend the excellent guide *Plant Protection in the Garden*. It should be on every gardener's bookshelf. (See under Recommended Reading.)

Diseases

A good number of plant diseases are specific to a given group or family e.g. Fire Blight, a bacterial disease which attacks members of the rose family (*Rosaceae*) entering through the flower clusters and causing the spur or shoot to die back leaving it in a shrivelled state as if blasted by a flame gun. Shrubs which can be affected this way include *Cotoneaster, Pyracantha* and *Photinia*. Affected branches should be removed and burned. If the disease persists then the whole shrub must be dug up and burned. Fire Blight disease, however, seems to be prevalent in some areas and absent or less common in others. It is not inevitable and fear of its appearance should not prevent you from growing these popular shrubs in your garden. Verticillium Wilt and Phytophthora are fungus diseases that attack through the roots of a range of shrubs causing foliage wilt and shoot die-back. The former is especially associated with *Cotinus, Rhus* and *Viburnum*. Normally, only odd branches are affected and these should be cut back to living wood and burned. Rarely are large shrubs killed outright. The soil around the shrub may be drenched with benomyl. Verticillium Wilt is usually found where intensive cultivation has been practised in the past and especially where potatoes have long been grown. Phytophthora causes a root rot and a progressive wilting of shoots leading to the death of *Rhododendron, Erica, Calluna* and some conifers. This disease is more likely to be found under certain nursery conditions than in the garden but recently acquired plants may sometimes be affected. Affected plants must be removed and burned as there is no control available. Young plants of these genera which suddenly collapse and die are most likely to have been the victims of Phytophthora. Being a soil-water borne disease it is less likely to be found on well drained sites.

Honey Fungus (*Armillaria*) is the most widespread fungus disease affecting ornamental shrubs (trees and other plants too) and is particularly prevalent in areas of former woodland. The characteristic honey-brown toadstools usually appear in clumps in autumn beneath a dead or dying shrub or tree or on the site of a buried stump. The black root-like rhizomorphs of the fungus attack the roots of its victim, change into fan-like belts of white mycelium and travel progressively in towards the stem collar eventually causing its death. A wide range of shrubs are susceptible to this disease especially rhododendrons, privets, roses and lilacs, while camellias appear to be less susceptible, if not immune. Infected plants should be dug out and burned and the soil changed before replanting. There are, however, various chemicals on the market which are claimed to offer some control if used early enough. These include Armillatox and Bray's Emulsion, while mixing a portion of copper carbonate in the compost or soil at planting time is claimed by some gardeners to give protection to newly planted shrubs in infected areas. Large infected stumps which are impractical to remove can be drenched with one of the above preparations taking great care not to splash surrounding vegetation. Alternatively, they can be isolated by encircling them with a trench up to 30cm (12in) deep.

One of the most versatile diseases is coral spot (*Nectraria cinnabarina*), a fungus which is commonly associated only with dead wood – twigs, branches, peasticks, etc. – but which is also said to be responsible for attacking healthy tissue causing die back and ultimately, in some cases, death. It can be found on a wide range of woody plants including maples, *Cercis, Elaeagnus* and magnolias. The wood of infected plants becomes slightly discoloured (greenish in maples) while the characteristic orangey-pink spore postules appear on the dead or dying wood. Coral spot is especially active during periods of warm, damp conditions. Unfortunately, there is no known cure beyond the usual hygiene, i.e. pruning away and burning any dead or dying branches, infected or not. Be sure, incidentally, to make any such cuts well below the dead, or infected portion into completely healthy wood. Given that coral spot enters a host through wounds, even small ones, these should be treated with a recommended fungicidal paint. This is especially important when pruning those shrubs known to be particularly susceptible. As a precaution after pruning diseased branches, it is worth wiping your knife or secateurs with a cloth soaked in formalin. This will kill any diseased tissue, sap or spores adhering to the blades.

Another widespread disease of shrubs is powdery mildew which, like the pest red spider mite, is especially prevalent during prolonged warm, dry periods. It shows itself as a fine grey deposit on the upper leaf surface, except in the case of rhododendrons where it is found mainly on the leaf undersurface causing a blotchy effect on the upper surface. There are a number of powdery mildewicides available and a programme of protection on young plants certainly is worth considering. Finally, read my comments regarding the publication *Plant Protection in the Garden* under Pest Control.

There is no doubt that shrubs under stress are more likely to attract pests and diseases than those which are strong and healthy. Shrubs which are suffering poor growth as a result of bad drainage, soil compaction, drought, soil deficiencies, especially of essential elements, frost damage, etc., offer little or no resistance to attack. Likewise, those shrubs suffering physical damage as a result of careless use of spades, machinery, etc. are more susceptible. One cannot stress too often the importance of choosing the right shrub for the right site and the benefits of good cultivation and after-care.

Recommended Reading

There have been more books written about shrubs than any other hardy garden plants. Here are a few I have found most useful.

Australian Native Plants, J.W. Wrigley and M. Fagg, 1979 (Collins)
For those able to grow these plants this book offers an excellent practical account.

Azaleas, Fred C. Gale, 1985 (Timber Press)
An expensive but comprehensive account, there is none better.

The Collingridge Dictionary of Plant Names, Allen J. Coombes, 1986
A most handy and useful guide to plant names; their spelling, meaning and pronunciation.

The Colour Dictionary of Camellias, Stirling Macoboy, 1981 (Landsdowne)
An alphabetical account of Camellia species, hybrids and cultivars, beautifully illustrated in colour.

The Cultivation of New Zealand Trees and Shrubs, L.J. Metcalf 1972 (Reed)
The best account of its kind, highly practical.

Dwarf Rhododendrons and *The Larger Species of Rhododendron*, both Peter A. Cox, 1973 and 1979 (Batsford)
Two lively and comprehensive accounts of Rhododendrons species in cultivation by one who grows and knows them.

Encyclopaedia of Australian Plants W.R. Elliot and D.L. Jones, 1980 onwards (Lothian)
Five volumes published with more to come. Expensive but invaluable. Comprehensive and well illustrated in colour.

Encyclopaedia of Rhododendron Hybrids Peter A. and Kenneth N. Cox, 1988 (Batsford)
Descriptions and assessments of almost 2,000 hybrid rhododendrons by two of Britain's best known experts on the subject.

Fuchsia Lexicon, R. Ewart, 2nd edn revised, 1987 (Blandford)
An alphabetical descriptive guide to some 2,000 fuchsias – species and cultivars – plus many colour photographs.

Gardens of England & Wales (The National Gardens Scheme)
Published annually, the *Yellow Book*, as it is fondly known, gives details of over 2,000 private gardens open to the public under the above scheme – a well known charitable trust. It is a must for the car, pocket or rucksack to be carried everywhere. Think of all those shrubs to be seen, noted and perhaps photographed. Many of these gardens also offer plants, including shrubs, for sale.

The Good Gardens Guide, edited by Graham Rose and Peter King, 1990 (Barrie & Jenkins)
The first of what is intended as an annual guide. It describes over 1,000 of the best gardens open to the public in Great Britain and Ireland. It is complementary to the *Yellow Book* (see above).

The Heather Garden, H.J. van de Laar, 1978 (Collins)
Probably the best of several similar works on this subject. This is an English translation of a very popular Dutch book.

Hilliers Manual of Trees and Shrubs, revised edn 1991 (David & Charles)
This has been called by some a mini Bean. Brief descriptions of over 8,000 woody plants, ideal for the gardener's pocket or bag.

Japanese Maples, J.D. Vertrees, 2nd edn 1987 (Timber Press)
The best English account of its kind written by a specialist grower. Well illustrated in colour.

Manual of Cultivated Broad-leaved Trees and Shrubs G. Krüssmann, 1984–6, English edn, 3 vols (Batsford).
An expensive but comprehensive work, illustrated throughout with black and white photographs and line drawings.

Manual of Cultivated Trees and Shrubs Hardy in North America, A. Rehder, 2nd edn 1947 (Dioscorides Press)
An American classic, equally applicable to the British Isles. For specialists and keen students.

Manual of Woody Landscape Plants, Michael Dirr, 1983 (Stipes)
A highly original and eminently practical account for American and British gardeners and landscapers. Full of common sense, personal experience and refreshing touches of humour.

The Plant Finder
An annual publication of the Hardy Plant Society giving the names of over 50,000 plants and their sources of supply.

Plant Protection in the Garden, edited by G.W. Ivens, J. Stubbs and the scientific staff of the Royal Horticultural Society, published jointly by the British Crop Protection Council and the RHS.
A timely account of the major pests, diseases and weeds in gardens and the best methods of controlling them with the appropriate chemicals.

The Pruning of Trees, Shrubs and Conifers, George E. Brown, 1972 (Faber)
The standard work on the subject based on the author's long experience at Kew and elsewhere.

Shrubs, Roger Phillips and Martyn Rix, 1989 (Pan)
A wealth of superb colour photographs plus brief descriptions and notes. An excellent aid to shrub identification.

The Tree and Shrub Expert, Dr D.G. Hessayon, 1983 (pbi Publications)
An excellent beginner's guide to the selection and care of trees, shrubs and conifers.

Trees and Shrubs Hardy in the British Isles, W.J. Bean, 8th edn 1970–88 (revised) edited by Desmond Clarke (John Murray)
Four volumes and a supplement by Desmond Clarke. Expensive, but for those specially interested in woody plants indispensable. Not for nothing is it known as the tree and shrub enthusiast's bible.

List of Suppliers

Achamore Gardens, Isle of Gigha, Argyll PA41 7AD

Ballalheannagh Gardens, Glen Roy, Lonan, Isle of Man.

F.G. Barcock & Co. Ltd, Garden House Farm, Drinkstone, Bury St. Edmunds, Suffolk IP30 9TN.

Blackthorn Nursery, Kilmeston, Alresford, Hampshire SO24 0NL.

Bluebell Nurseries, Blackfordby, Nr Burton-on-Trent, Staffordshire DE11 8AJ.

Bodnant Garden Nursery Ltd, Tal-y-Cafn, Colwyn Bay, Clwyd LL28 5RE.

Bridgemere Nurseries, Bridgemere, Nr. Nantwich, Cheshire CW5 7QB

Burncoose and Southdown Nurseries, Gwennap, Redruth, Cornwall TR16 6BJ.

Cannington College Plant Centre, Cannington, Bridgwater, Somerset TA5 2LS.

Chiltern Seeds, Bortree Stile, Ulverston, Cumbria LA12 7DP (seeds).

Costin's Nurseries, Portgloriam, Kilcock, Co. Kildare, Republic of Ireland.

County Park Nursery, Essex Gardens, Hornchurch, Essex RM11 3BU.

The Dairies (James Russell), Castle Howard, York, Yorkshire.

Daisy Hill Nurseries Ltd, Hospital Road, Newry, Co. Down, N. Ireland BT35 8PN.

Edrom Nurseries, Coldingham, Eyemouth, Berwickshire TD14 5TZ.

Exbury Enterprises Ltd, Exbury, Nr Southampton, Hampshire SO4 1AZ.

The Fortescue Garden Trust, The Garden House, Buckland Monachorum, Yelverton, Devon PL20 7LQ.

Glendoick Gardens Ltd, Glendoick, Perth, Scotland PH2 7NS.

Goscote Nurseries Ltd, Syston Road, Cossington, Leicestershire LE7 8NZ.

Green Farm Plants, Green Farm, Bentley, Farnham, Surrey GU10 5JX.

Hergest Croft Gardens, Kington, Herefordshire HR5 3GE.

Hillier Nurseries (Winchester) Ltd, Ampfield House, Ampfield, Romsey, Hampshire SO5 9PA.

Holden Clough Nursery, Holden, Bolton-by-Bowland, Clitheroe, Lancashire BB7 4PF.

Hopleys Plants Ltd, High Street, Much Hadham, Hertfordshire SG10 6BU.

Hydon Nurseries, Clockbarn Lane, Hydon Heath, Nr Godalming, Surrey GU8 4AZ.

W.E. Th. Ingwersen Ltd, Birch Farm Nursery, Gravetye, East Grinstead, West Sussex RH19 4LE.

Knightshayes Garden Trust, Knightshayes Court, Tiverton, Devon EX16 7RG.

Langley Boxwood Nursery, Langley Court, Liss, Hampshire GU33 7JL.

Langthorn's Plantery, High Cross, North Walsham, Norfolk NR28 0DR.

Lea Rhododendron Gardens Ltd, Lea, Matlock, Derbyshire DE4 5GH.

Longstock Park Nursery, Longstock, Nr Stockbridge, Hampshire SO20 6EH.

Macpenny's, 154 Bransgore, Christchurch, Dorset BH23 8DB.

Mallet Court Nursery, Mallet Court, Curry Mallet, Taunton, Somerset TA3 6SY.

Marwood Hill (Dr J. Smart), Barnstaple, Devon EX31 4EB.

Nangle's Nursery, Carrigrohane, Cork, Republic of Ireland.

Notcutts Nurseries, Woodbridge, Suffolk IP12 4AF.

Penwood Nurseries (Mr and Mrs D. Harris), Penwood, Old Burghclere, Nr Newbury, Berkshire.

Raveningham Hall Gardens, Norwich, Norfolk NR14 0NS.

G. Reuthe Ltd, Jackass Lane, Keston, Kent BR2 6AW.

Royal Horticultural Society Garden, Rosemoor, Great Torrington, Devon EX38 8PH.

Savill Garden Plant Centre, Savill Garden, Windsor, Berkshire SL4 2HT.

Seaforde Gardens, Seaforde, Co. Down, N. Ireland.

Spinners, Boldre, Lymington, Hampshire SO41 5QE.

Starborough Nursery, Starborough Road, Marsh Green, Edenbridge, Kent TN8 5RB.

Stone House Cottage Nurseries, Stone, Nr Kidderminster, Worcestershire DY10 4BG.

Sussex County Gardens, Newhaven Road, Kingston, Nr. Lewes, East Sussex BN7 3NE.

Treasures of Tenbury Ltd, Burford House, Tenbury Wells, Worcestershire WR15 8HQ.

Trehane Camellia Nursery, Stapehill Road, Hampreston, Wimborne, Dorset BH21 7NE.

Trewithen Nurseries, Grampound Road, Truro, Cornwall.

Wisley Plant Sales Centre, RHS Garden, Wisley, Woking, Surrey GU23 6QB.

Index

Figures in italics refer to illustrations

Picture Credits

HarperCollins Publishers would like to thank the author and those listed below for granting permission to publish the photographs featured in this book:
A–Z Botanical Collection 28
Heather Angel 148
Ardea Photographics 100, 160
Gillian Beckett 40
Eric Crichton Photos 20, 47, 92, 151
Ron & Christine Foord 27
The Garden Picture Library 107, 136
Andrew Lawson 109, 154
S & O Mathews 8 & 9, 134–5
Tania Midgley 70, 96, 99, 139
Photos Horticultural Picture Library 33, 49, 51, 93, 111, 125, 133, 156, 158, 163
Harry Smith Collection 2, 31, 39, 149
All other photographs were taken by the author